YORK NOTES

Learning Resource Centre
Park Road, Uxbridge Middlesex UB8 1NQ
Renewals: 01895 853326 Enquiries: 01895 853344

Please return this item to the Learning Centre on or before this last date
Stamped below:

1 1 JAN 2010

- 9 FEB 2010

3 0 SEP 2015

1 2 OCT 2015

823.8

DRACULA

BRAM STOKER

NOTES BY STEVE ROBERTS

UXBRIDGE COLLEGE
LEARNING CENTRE
WITHDRAWN

 Longman

York Press

The right of Steve Roberts to be identified as Author of this Work has
been asserted by him in accordance with the Copyright, Designs and
Patents Act 1988

YORK PRESS
322 Old Brompton Road, London SW5 9JH

PEARSON EDUCATION LIMITED
Edinburgh Gate, Harlow,
Essex CM20 2JE, United Kingdom
Associated companies, branches and representatives throughout the world

© Librairie du Liban *Publishers* 2006

All rights reserved. No part of this publication may be reproduced, stored
in a retrieval system, or transmitted in any form or by any means, electronic,
mechanical, photocopying, recording, or otherwise, without either the prior
written permission of the Publishers or a licence permitting restricted copying
in the United Kingdom issued by the Copyright Licensing Agency Ltd,
90 Tottenham Court Road, London W1T 4LP

First published 2006
Third Impression 2008

ISBN: 978–1–405–83566–4

Typeset by Pantek Arts Ltd, Maidstone, Kent
Printed in China

CONTENTS

PART FOUR

PART FIVE

PART ONE

INTRODUCTION

HOW TO STUDY A NOVEL

Studying a novel on your own requires self-discipline and a carefully thought-out work plan in order to be effective.

- You will need to read the novel more than once. Start by reading it quickly for pleasure, then read it slowly and thoroughly.

- On your second reading make detailed notes on the plot, characters and **themes** of the novel. Further readings will generate new ideas and help you to memorise the details of the story.

- Some of the characters will develop as the plot unfolds. How do your responses towards them change during the course of the novel?

- Think about how the novel is narrated. From whose point of view are events described?

- A novel may or may not present events chronologically: the time scheme may be a key to its structure and organisation.

- What part do the settings play in the novel?

- Are words, images or incidents repeated so as to give the work a pattern? Do such patterns help you to understand the novel's themes?

- Identify what styles of language are used in the novel.

- What is the effect of the novel's ending? Is the action completed and closed, or left incomplete and open?

- Does the novel present a moral and just world?

- Cite exact sources for all quotations, whether from the text itself or from critical commentaries. Wherever possible find your own examples from the novel to back up your opinions.

- Always express your ideas in your own words.

These York Notes offer an introduction to *Dracula* and cannot substitute for close reading of the text and the study of secondary sources.

CHECK THE BOOK

Michael McKeon's *Theory of the Novel: A Historical Approach* (2000) is an excellent introduction to the history of the novel.

CHECK THE BOOK

A Beginner's Guide to Critical Reading: Readings for Students by Richard Jacobs (2001) provides entertaining commentary on a range of literary texts. It will help you see how criticism and theory can enhance your own enjoyment and appreciation of literature.

READING *DRACULA*

'I suppose that every book of the kind must contain some lesson, but I prefer that readers should find it out for themselves,' said Bram Stoker, when interviewed in July 1897 about his new novel *Dracula*.

Authors are often asked to give a public account of their purpose in creating their text, and some are brave or foolish enough to do so. Where the author is unavailable for comment, there is usually no shortage of substitutes willing to testify to the author's true intentions. Whether Bram Stoker's remark reveals his authorial purpose or not, the idea that readers create their own personal interpretations of the text is reflected in his creative method. His reluctant acknowledgement of the 'lesson' inevitably contained in his text seems evasive. But the ambiguity of the remark is completely in line with the 'lesson' of *Dracula*. Many different readings can illuminate this remarkable novel, but the conflicts and tensions beneath the surface of the text do not resolve themselves into tidy explanations. The novel revolves around the question of how we can know what is true in our selves and the world we inhabit. The philosophical conflict between the religious and the scientific answers to that question is uneasily reconciled. As the ancient and modern world outlooks collide in the novel, Stoker's voice and perspective do not intrude directly. He expects the reader to find the lesson in his story. This is one reason, though not the only one, why this text is so open to interpretation.

There have been many different critical readings of the novel over the last three decades. Some commentaries take Mina Harker's unmarried name, Murray, as a reference to Anglo-Irish relations and see the Harkers' relationship as an extended **metaphor** for the relationship between Ireland and Britain. Stoker's family background is used to support this sort of reading. Others have found evidence of anti-Semitic tendencies in the description of Dracula's features. Is there a connection to Stoker's own possible marital frustrations in this novel? Does the biographical debate about whether or not syphilis was the real cause of Stoker's death illuminate in any way the novel's view of women? While it is intriguing to consider such possibilities, the reliability of any reading of the novel has to be founded in the text itself. Stoker's 'possible impossibilities' (Chapter 14, p. 160) provide a great deal of room for speculation.

CHECK THE BOOK

For an incredibly thorough and minutely referenced argument on the relevance of Ireland in *Dracula* see Joseph Valente's *Dracula's Crypt: Bram Stoker, Irishness, and the Question of Blood* (2002).

Dracula has never been out of print since its publication in 1897. It is surprising that a book with little immediate critical approval, by an author considered to be a minor literary figure, is so readily available to the public over one hundred years after its first imprint. Most modern critics do not dwell on the literary merit or demerit of Stoker's writing, skipping over the form in their pursuit of their perspective on the content. In imagining the vampire as Count Dracula, Stoker created a monster that is a metaphor for conscious and unconscious fears. He is the **archetypical** demon of the medieval age, modernised in the age of industrial revolution. The vampire has escaped from Stoker's book and been resurrected many times on the screen. This has contributed to the book's longevity, but the visual **imagery** the book has inspired only partly explains the enduring position of Count Dracula in the mainstream of our culture.

Consider how *Dracula* shapes our understanding of the ancient myths of vampirism. Stoker gathered diverse sources together to make the legend, adding many of the details we now regard as the typical characteristics of ancient vampires. A wealth of detail from history and folklore was derived from his years of background research, but the title, *Dracula*, was a last-minute revision. There are few novels where the character whose name provides the title of the book is given so little direct contact with the reader. Count Dracula casts no reflection and, after the first few chapters, is seldom seen in his own form. Who or what do we see when we look at him in the novel? Despite this elusive quality, *Dracula* exists in many forms beyond its pages. In children's and adults' books, cartoons, films, computer games and music, the vampire legend continues to exercise its fascination.

Unlike the monster in Mary Shelley's *Frankenstein, or The Modern Prometheus*, Dracula is not an accident or an experiment. He is the product of a man's pursuit of power and knowledge. Dracula chooses his own fate. There are links with so many myths and legends that it is almost arbitrary to mention any particular influence in this introduction. The Greek myth of Prometheus, who stole fire from the gods and suffered a terrible fate, can be seen in both *Frankenstein* and *Dracula*. Shelley sets her hero in the Promethean mould, challenging the gods for the power of life and death. Stoker's villain volunteered to become a monster that negates life and death.

CONTEXT

Vampire legends are found in various forms in many different cultures. It is not a defining feature of East European mythology, though *Dracula* did much to establish that link.

 CHECK THE BOOK

Mary Shelley's *Frankenstein* (1818), although generally considered a Gothic novel, does not observe the established **conventions** of the **genre**.

Whereas Frankenstein is appalled by his creation, Dracula revels in his inhumanity. These two characters became cinematic icons in the early decades of film-making, but it is Dracula who has had the more lasting impact on the language and conventions of film, both within and beyond the genre of the horror movie.

CHECK THE FILM

Friedrich Wilhelm Murnau's critically acclaimed *Nosferatu* (1922) was 'adapted from the novel by Bram Stoker' by Henrik Galeen. Stoker's widow took legal action against this unauthorised version of *Dracula* and all copies were supposed to be destroyed. Fortunately copies survived.

Dracula has an established cinematic presence in numerous film adaptations: the German Expressionist *Nosferatu* in 1922; the Hollywood version with Bela Lugosi in 1931; the many British horror pictures by Hammer Films between 1958 and 1974; the Francis Ford Coppola epic *Bram Stoker's Dracula* in 1992; and many others. Stoker's **theme** of civilisation threatened by terror often reoccurs in the science fiction film genre. The villains and monsters in *Star Wars* or *Alien* share some traits, at least, with the Count.

The novel anticipates the coming modern age, and also postmodernist relativism, but in the exhausted literary form of a bygone era. As a narrative entertainment, *Dracula* exploits the conventions of the ghost story. The question of life after death, the existence of the soul and the possibility of communication with the dead are all accepted for the purposes of the story. Stoker's use of the conventional elements of the Gothic novel – the supernatural, the dark ruins, the madness – brings his story into a genre that was considered **melodramatic** and out of fashion. This may account for the **ambivalence** in the critical appreciation of the novel, both then and now. But Stoker's work in the theatre would have given him an awareness of the popular appeal of melodrama.

Stoker's tale seems to offer the consolation of religious and moral certainties in an uncertain world. The triumph of good over evil represents a hopeful ideal for the preservation of civilised society. The modern world is seen as fresh and exciting but useful only within a conservative recognition of older values. Unsurprisingly, this 'lesson' can be read in many different ways.

CHECK THE NET

For a comprehensive film database listing *Dracula* cinematic adaptations, search the Internet Movie Database at **www.imdb.com**

Stoker goes to some lengths to present this work of fantasy as true. This is one of the dominant themes within the novel: the construction of meaning and the interpretation of truth. While Stoker's display of modern gadgetry reminds readers of today that technological innovation is not a new phenomenon, his focus on the modern means of communication is significant. The end of the nineteenth century was a time of reflection and apprehension. The British Empire was in competition with other empires and the future was uncertain. Enormous social changes were taking place in British society, challenging the accepted social hierarchy. The expanded participation in democracy, the introduction of mass education and the small but significant improvement in women's rights were all indications of progress profoundly unsettling for some. The developments in industry, science and philosophy were equally challenging. The transformations in this novel, embodied in the women and in the shape-shifter Dracula, are grotesque metaphors for the social and personal transformations in late Victorian society. While our concerns and fears may reflect a variety of values, forms and priorities, many of the terrors of the Victorian age are still relevant to a twenty-first-century readership.

Is the postmodern age so different? Superstition, religion and science still coexist in our culture despite a less overt adherence to the Christian faith. For many people, the fundamental questions of existence are still unanswerable. Dracula embodies the fear of the unknown and he **personifies** the 'nothing in the darkness' that keeps children awake at night. What would it be like to live for ever: a blessing or a curse? What would it mean to cheat death by stealing life from others, only to survive by parasitic dependence on lesser mortals?

The sexual appeal and repulsiveness of the vampire has ensured a certain level of prurient interest in subsequent adaptations. Whether the novel is a metaphor for the contradictory nature of human sexuality, an extended **exposition** of the nature of the soul, an **allegory** of colonial domination or a reaction to the emancipation of women, it still works as a romantic fantasy adventure. Stoker was concerned with creating a good story. The novel's success, however shocking or titillating its moments of excitement, rests on its merits as an adventure. It reflects the historical period in which it was written. It is more relevant to remember the Victorian era as an age of enquiry into the issues of the human mind than as an era of sexual hypocrisy. While it is true that nude statues in the Crystal

CHECK THE BOOK

Lord Byron's poem *The Giaour*, published in 1813, is often considered one of the early examples of vampire literature. In it he writes: 'But first, on earth as Vampire sent, / Thy corse shall from its tomb be rent: / Then ghastly haunt thy native place, / And suck the blood of all thy race'.

Palace Great Exhibition in 1851 were thought so scandalous they had to be amended with strategic fig leaves, and the Obscene Publications Act of 1857 brought the word 'pornography' into the legal language of Britain, the issue of sexual identity in Victorian society is more complex than such repressive measures might tend to suggest.

The main characters and their virtues are depicted most clearly in the final **tableau** as the positive idealisation of the petit bourgeois or 'middle-class' extended family. This happy ending models the social trend in the middle class for smaller families with fewer children. The 'lesson' is an endorsement of Mina Harker as the personification of the Victorian ideals of motherhood and the good woman. Even in Stoker's time, this would not have explained the novel's appeal to readers. The powerful image of the Count, the sexy seducer who can make women do whatever he wants, is not diminished by the moralising **tone** of the set-piece ending.

In terms of the novel as romantic adventure, Mina and Jonathan Harker's relationship forms the central love story: they meet temptations and dangers, they are separated for much of the novel, yet they are united and enjoy a happy ending. Their voices are also important to the telling of the novel: Jonathan Harker speaks to us at greater length than Mina but they contribute the majority of the narrative between them. In terms of the other characters, almost half the story is told by Dr Jack Seward; Dr Van Helsing, though so central to the action, addresses the reader as **narrator** less than Lucy Westenra; Arthur Holmwood (later Lord Godalming) and Quincey Morris add little to the narrative in their own right; and Dracula writes only a short note of welcome to Jonathan on his arrival in Transylvania. So whose story is this?

Does this novel have much to say to a modern audience? The reality of family life in Britain certainly looks nothing like the ideal picture at the end of Stoker's novel. The twenty-first century could be said to have inherited a version of the Victorian 'double standard' on sexuality and gender identities. Is the open display of female sexuality, an aspect of 'girl power', less threatening now than it was in 1897? Stoker's much overworked word 'voluptuous' could easily

CONTEXT

Novels in the Gothic genre often make use of the possible confusions and interpretations presented to the reader by telling the story from more than one character's point of view. The reader then has to negotiate a range of possible interpretations as part of the reading of the story itself. The events of the story are distanced from the reader, who realises, to a lesser or greater extent, that the narrator may not be a totally reliable witness. This ambiguity of meaning is introduced deliberately and exploited by the author for a variety of effects.

be applied to images of the female in modern media texts. Is the so-called 'raunch' culture a form of liberation or exploitation?

The central metaphor of humanity risking its own destruction through a failure of understanding is still potent, though we may see our world more at risk from environmental catastrophe than social evils. Nevertheless, Dracula is often seen as a cipher for the spread of sexually transmitted disease. Now, as in the Victorian age, prostitution is an issue that most countries are struggling to deal with effectively. The media in Britain, when reporting high levels of teenage pregnancy, an increase in sexually transmitted infections, or HIV and Aids, cannot discuss sexual health and education without causing moral panic. The Internet, our new form of communication, presents challenging issues of censorship and freedom of expression. The economic gap between men and women in Britain is not as large as it was, but it is still there. Is motherhood less idealised in this age? Stoker's happy ending may or may not be an ideal we would adopt, but the 'lesson' of *Dracula* raises many questions that remain difficult and provocative.

CHECK THE NET
The text of *Dracula* is available online at **www.online-literature.com**; this is useful if you wish to search for specific phrases or key words.

PART TWO

THE TEXT

NOTE ON THE TEXT

 CHECK THE NET
The All Things Dracula website at **www.cesnur.org/2003/dracula** has some detailed historical background on the various editions and adaptations of *Dracula*, including a full bibliography of the editions.

The edition of *Dracula* used in these Notes is the 2000 imprint of the Wordsworth Classics edition by Wordsworth Editions Limited. This version of the novel is based on the text published in Britain in 1897 by Archibald Constable. While there are few significant changes in the edition published later in America in 1899, some minor textual details give scope for variety in interpretation. Differences between Stoker's preparatory notes and a surviving typewritten manuscript suggest that a number of changes, including the title of the novel, were made very close to the date of first publication. A significant change was the omission of a passage on the destruction of Castle Dracula at the end of the novel.

SYNOPSIS

Dracula is a compilation of eyewitness accounts and various forms of reportage that tells the story of Jonathan and Mina Harker's experiences in Transylvania and England at the end of the nineteenth century. Their relationship endures through separation, madness and a range of seductions. They are tested by their adventures, but survive to enjoy a happy marriage at the end. Their story, related by a variety of friends and strangers, is bound up with the story of the monster that threatens them: Count Dracula.

As the novel opens, solicitor Jonathan Harker travels from London to Transylvania to assist Count Dracula in his preparations to move to England. He enjoys, at first, the novelty of the strange land, the almost barbarous people and their superstitious customs. His journey is a sequence of bizarre and 'uncanny' incidents. He becomes less confident when he arrives at Castle Dracula and realises he is effectively a prisoner. Count Dracula uses Jonathan to learn about the new world he plans to invade. Jonathan discovers many things about Count Dracula and tries unsuccessfully to communicate with the outside world.

His fears are confirmed during an interrupted encounter with three vampire women. Dracula promises his vampires shall have Harker when the time comes. When Dracula leaves for England, Jonathan makes a desperate escape from the castle, knowing his fate is sealed.

In England, Jonathan's fiancée, Mina Murray, and her companion, Lucy Westenra, are looking forward to their forthcoming marriages. Lucy has recently become engaged to an English aristocrat, Arthur Holmwood. Two of his closest friends, Dr John Seward and an American, Quincey Morris, also love her, but she has refused their marriage proposals. Mina and Lucy enjoy a stay in Whitby, but are disturbed by some strange premonitions from local people. A gathering storm threatens the coast, and the gloomy ruins of the abbey add to a sense of impending doom.

Dracula arrives by ship and Lucy becomes one of his first English victims. She returns home to the south of England, and there seems to recover. Dracula establishes himself in another old ruin near an asylum for the insane. The asylum is run by Dr Seward, who takes a particular interest in one of the mental patients, Renfield. It becomes clear that Renfield's erratic behaviour and penchant for blood are linked to the arrival of Dracula.

Finally Mina hears news of Jonathan, and goes abroad to nurse him. There he and Mina marry as Lucy's health deteriorates. Under the guidance of Dr Van Helsing, Lucy's friends give their blood to save her, but in vain. Lucy becomes a vampire and is destroyed by her fiancé, Arthur, now Lord Godalming following the death of his father.

Dr Van Helsing contacts Mina Harker and she shares with him her husband's secret journal of his time in Transylvania. The men gain a better understanding of their enemy and prepare to track down the vampire. As the men enter his lair, Dracula attacks Mina and threatens to enslave her. Jonathan is distressed by his wife's suffering, but she inspires him and the other men with her steadfast courage. The men bravely ambush Count Dracula in his London house and Dracula is forced to abandon his plans and return to Transylvania.

> **CONTEXT**
> Stoker first started researching and making notes for *Dracula* on 8 March 1890, while holidaying in Whitby.

The men pursue Dracula across Europe. Dr Van Helsing enters Castle Dracula and destroys the lair of Dracula and the three vampire women. Dracula is stopped on the road near his castle and, after a desperate struggle, is defeated. Mina Harker is released from the vampire's curse; Quincey Morris sacrifices his life for her safety. The story ends seven years later with Mina and Jonathan Harker reflecting on their incredible adventures in the company of Dr Van Helsing.

DETAILED SUMMARIES

A NOTE

GLOSSARY

2 **manifest** obvious, easily understood

2 **variance** a point of difference or conflict

2 **contemporary** at the same time

- An anonymous note stands as preface to the story.
- The story is presented as historical fact, from a chosen sequence of 'papers'.
- The story, though beyond belief, is based on reliable accounts of experience.

An anonymous note informs readers that the question of how the story came to be presented in this way will become clear. The note assures readers that the 'papers' are the essential highlights of extensive personal experiences and should be regarded as reliable evidence of simple historical facts.

COMMENTARY

The novel begins with a question mark over the identity of the **narrator**. This is immediately unsettling and undermines the assurances of clarification and authenticity. The **tone** is understated, hinting at some awful horror to come, yet at the same time seems rather secretarial in its intent. The author of the note asks us to tolerate the organisation of the following 'papers' (p. 2). We are assured that the significance of their sequence will become obvious. The use of the term 'papers' suggests an objective or scientific weight of authenticity that other words for writing or records do not necessarily convey. We are told that the 'papers' are the essential selection presenting a true historical record. The note's author asks for our belief in the story but warns us that the tale will not match our usual thinking about the world. Our incredulity is also forestalled by the note's assertion that there is no possibility of error in the accounts compiled. All the accounts have been selected because they were written at the time of the events by witnesses. We are asked to accept that these are matters of fact, uncorrupted by imagination or unreliable memory.

Who wrote the note? Who compiled the records of this 'history'? The identity of the author of this note will be revealed later in the narrative, but at this point it is withheld. In fact, it will not become completely clear until Chapter 17, at the start of the third phase of the novel. It is a teasing question as we are drawn, from the start, into a mysterious affair by a stranger who, anticipating and understanding our disbelief, gently insists there can be no mistake.

> **CONTEXT**
>
> The epistolary novel is a story told mostly or entirely through messages written by one character to another. The reader is put in the position of a detective, spying on the private communication of the characters and deducing the story from partial information.

CHAPTER 1

- Jonathan Harker keeps detailed notes of his journey from London to Transylvania.
- On St George's Day, Jonathan is collected by the Count's driver and travels on alone.
- Jonathan sees strange blue flames and is threatened by wolves.
- He is gripped by a dreadful fear as they arrive at Castle Dracula.

Jonathan Harker keeps his journal as a record of his travels in the eastern parts of Europe, and it is clear he intends this journal to be read by a woman he refers to in a very familiar manner as Mina. He complains of late-running trains before mentioning the unusual food eaten along the way. He later blames the food for a disturbed and uneasy night of restless dreams.

GLOSSARY

5 **diligence** from the eighteenth-century French *carrosse de diligence*, which means 'coach of speed'

6 **idolatrous** adjective formed from the noun 'idolatry' – the worship of false gods or idols

7 **cat's-meat** horse meat prepared on skewers to feed domestic cats

10 **calèche** a light carriage with a removable folding hood

CONTEXT

The rowan tree – also known as the mountain ash – is considered in occult lore to be a protection against enchantment. The wild rose is associated with Catholic traditions; it is said that priests' rosary beads were made of rose hips as their colour **symbolised** the blood of Christ.

Jonathan explains how he prepared for his journey by researching in the British Museum: he is working with 'a noble of that country' and does not wish to appear ignorant. He is to meet with Count Dracula at his castle in 'one of the wildest and least known portions of Europe' (p. 3).

Harker's knowledge of the peoples of the region introduces a hint of their terrible history. He comments loftily on the 'imaginative whirlpool' that has gathered 'every known superstition in the world' into this region and reminds himself twice to ask the Count about these matters (p. 4). He relishes the history of the region as a site of conflict, war and bloodshed, because it adds some excitement to his adventure into unknown and possibly dangerous lands.

Almost everything is 'picturesque' to Jonathan (p. 4). He enjoys making this record of his travels and jokes about the deceptive attractions of the women of the region. He is clearly aware of the female form as he comments on his elderly landlady's apron being 'almost too tight for modesty' (p. 5).

He records a polite note from the Count welcoming him to the Carpathians. The Count also instructs him to 'Sleep well tonight' (p. 5), though Harker does not comment on the **irony** of this given his disturbed sleep the night before.

As he draws near to the Count's home, Jonathan becomes aware of the people's strange reluctance to communicate. No one will answer his questions about the Count. His landlady warns him that it is the eve of St George's Day, a night when, at the stroke of midnight, 'all the evil things in the world will have full sway'. After failing to persuade him to postpone or abandon his journey, she places a rosary around his neck. Harker is sufficiently affected by her emotional appeal to overcome his own religious scruples as 'an English Churchman' about wearing such a symbol (p. 6).

As he sets off in the coach, Jonathan is aware that he is being talked about by the people around him. He does not appreciate their pitying looks, nor does he fully understand the nature of their conversation. He has only been able to translate a few words: 'Satan', 'hell', 'witch', 'were-wolf or vampire' (p. 7). A passenger reluctantly explains the people's odd gestures as a sign to guard against 'the evil eye'. Jonathan is touched by this odd combination of religious and superstitious concern for his well-being, despite its unpleasant impact on his feelings.

Jonathan describes in greater detail the beauty of the scenery he is leaving behind as he moves towards his rendezvous with the Count's coach. He notes the unhealthy appearance of the peasants that they pass. The coach climbs the rough road into the hills as the sun begins to set, and the coachman says that Harker may soon learn the dangers of wild animals. As night falls, his journey becomes a frenzied dash. His fellow passengers urge the driver to speed crazily along the road. They also give a puzzled Harker some 'odd and varied' gifts with many kind words and blessings (p. 9).

On arriving an hour early at the appointed place, the coachman urges Harker to return another day. Immediately, the Count's coach appears out of the darkness, and the driver takes Harker away from the terrified passengers. The landscape disappears under snow and Jonathan hears wolves howling. He notices with a shock that it is now midnight. He is startled by strange blue flames and baffled by the driver's odd behaviour: not only does the driver seem to be taking him around in circles, he keeps leaving the coach to follow the blue lights. Harker has the strange notion that he can see the light of the flames right through the driver's body. Abandoned by the driver, Jonathan realises the coach is surrounded by wolves and is paralysed with fear. The coachman seems to have a strange ability to command the animals. The coach stops, at last, in the moonlit courtyard of a dark, ruined castle.

CONTEXT

As 'an English Churchman', a Protestant, it is interesting, and odd in many ways, that Jonathan Harker should be reminded of 'old missals' when he sees certain 'little towns or castles on the top of steep hills' (p. 4). A missal is an old form of illustrated prayer book particularly associated with the Roman Catholic Church, typically containing the service of the Mass for the whole year.

COMMENTARY

Jonathan Harker's journal is the first 'paper' presented to the reader. The chapter heading notes the original has been kept in shorthand, therefore this account has been transcribed by someone. Could this be the same person who wrote the note preceding the chapter?

Jonathan's journal, written from the perspective of an English gentleman abroad, begins in the informal personal style of a typical traveller's monologue: part diary and part memoir. Comments on the incompetence of foreign railways and the strangeness of foreign food help to emphasise the notion that Harker is encountering the strange and unfamiliar. This is an **ironic** preparation for entering the realm of the entirely unknown. For Stoker's audience, the West represented civilisation and security; the East was an unspecified place of barbarous uncertainty and exotic adventure. Nevertheless, the Far East, the Middle East and the Near East were of strategic importance to the British Empire. Eastern Europe, on the other hand, represented the hinterland between things known and things foreign. Stoker makes use of this sense of a mysterious place to undermine the certainties of civilised existence.

Jonathan Harker's complaints of train delays do more than inform us of the tedious length of his journey. Time, an important aspect of civilised and organised society, is of lesser significance in the East. Jonathan cannot locate Castle Dracula on any map. He is operating in a world where the usual constraints of space and time are no longer reliable.

The **metaphorical** associations of the journey he records are equally clear. He moves away from his home, domestic bliss (represented by Mina) and order; and he heads towards an unknown destination, uncomfortable isolation and chaos. He leaves beauty, pity and warmth behind as he moves towards danger, cruelty and coldness. His innocent intentions to ask the Count about the superstitious beliefs of the people act as an ironic counterpoint to his increasing sense of unease. The second entry in his journal concludes with a

CHECK THE BOOK

Emily Brontë's *Wuthering Heights* (1847) features a violent and destructive male character of uncertain origin.

remark that foreshadows the events of the narrative: 'If this book should ever reach Mina before I do, let it bring my good-bye' (p. 6).

Stoker has also established a connection early in his narrative between sleeplessness, uneasy dreaming and the Count. The Count's remark – 'Sleep well tonight' – in the note to Jonathan is, at one level, an innocent pleasantry from a host to his guest (p. 5). When we consider the possibility that the Count might know of Harker's troubled and restless night, it becomes a rather more sinister matter. A similar sense of threat arises when the Count's driver speaks to the other coachman with full knowledge of a conversation he could not have overheard. This also raises the question of the identity of the person who collects Harker in the Count's coach.

Harker's innocence allows the reader a sense of irony. Although he speaks other languages and has prepared for his trip abroad, he is not able to communicate with those who might be able to warn him. He does not appreciate the significance of their concern. He does notice that rather a lot of people seem to have some injury to their necks. The most grimly humorous example of this naivety is his inability to distinguish between the words 'were-wolf or vampire' in translation (p. 7). His dictionary, another usually reliable source, seems unclear. Harker's confusion contributes to the vague and unformed menace that fuels his fears. In a very real sense, he is approaching his doom like a lamb to the slaughter.

> **CONTEXT**
>
> Jonathan Harker comments as they pass 'Cszeks and Slovaks, all in picturesque attire … that goitre was painfully prevalent' (p. 8). A goitre is a dangerous swelling of the thyroid gland in the neck.

CHAPTER 2

- Jonathan Harker meets Count Dracula.
- Jonathan assists Count Dracula with his plans to move to London.
- He notices the Count has no reflection in a mirror.
- Jonathan realises he is a prisoner in Castle Dracula.

GLOSSARY

14 **traps** luggage, baggage and belongings; possibly an early nineteenth-century shortening of 'trappings'

20 **myriad** derived from the Greek, literally meaning 'ten thousand', it is more often understood to suggest a very large number

23 **diffuse** confused or incoherent – here a writing style that lacks focus

Jonathan Harker arrives in the courtyard of Castle Dracula. He describes the massive doorway, and notices the strength of the coach driver. He is welcomed by Count Dracula, who escorts him to his room and explains the absence of servants at this late hour. The Count seems to be an attentive host, ensuring that Jonathan has food, wine and a cigar, but takes none of these pleasures himself.

Jonathan describes the Count, emphasising his pale skin and hairy hands. He also notes the 'horrible feeling of nausea' that comes over him, which he thinks may be caused by Count Dracula's bad breath. Wolves howl in the darkness, to the Count's delight; he remarks that as a city dweller Harker cannot 'enter into the feelings of the hunter' (p. 17). Jonathan refers in his journal to the uneasy thoughts he experiences as he goes to bed.

Count Dracula does not appear in the daytime and Jonathan hesitantly explores some of the castle alone. He notes the obvious wealth displayed, and spots there are no mirrors in the place. After encountering a locked door, he finds a library and a lot of familiar English books. Count Dracula joins Harker in the library and discusses his plans to move to England; he explains he has been studying England through books for years, but now wishes to learn more about the English tongue from his guest. The Count allows Harker to explore the castle, with the reservation that some doors will be locked, and reminds him that Transylvania's customs are strange to the outsider. Jonathan takes the opportunity to question his host about the mystery of the blue lights he saw on his journey. Count Dracula speaks of the troubled history of the region and how the superstitious peasants believe the lights mark hidden treasure.

Jonathan and Dracula talk through the night again. The Count asks Harker to tell him about the new home in England. Harker describes the Carfax estate in Purfleet. The fact that the house is old pleases Count Dracula, who talks of his wish to be alone with his thoughts among the shadows. At daybreak the Count suddenly retires.

CONTEXT

In 1897 Transylvania was a Hungarian province. After the First World War it became part of Romania.

The next day, as he is shaving, Jonathan is surprised by Dracula, and realises that the Count casts no reflection in the shaving mirror. Jonathan is so startled he cuts himself with his razor. Dracula reaches out furiously, but draws back at the touch of the crucifix around Harker's throat. Dracula throws the mirror out of the window.

Later, Jonathan discovers that all the doors leading out of the castle are locked and realises he is a prisoner.

COMMENTARY

Castle Dracula is a 'remarkable place' (p. 14), with its courtyard of dark arches and massive carved stone entrance. Jonathan finds himself abandoned at the entrance to a forbidding, ancient and time-weathered building. The castle is a closed, hostile fortress; visitors are neither expected nor accommodated: there is no way for him to attract attention. The imposing architecture has an intimidating impact on Harker. He has to remind himself of his newly acquired professional status as an act of reassurance: a solicitor's clerk might be intimidated by such a 'grim adventure', but not a fully qualified solicitor (p. 14). Jonathan finds it all difficult to believe. Is he awake or is this all a dream? The notions of an uncertain reality, the confusion of conscious and unconscious and the reliability of our senses are by now an established motif of the novel.

> **CONTEXT**
>
> The ruined castle is a typical location of the Gothic **genre** and Stoker's description here goes some way towards connecting the literary and architectural **conventions** of the Gothic tradition.

The chapter begins with Jonathan awaiting admittance at the entrance to Castle Dracula. This **symbolically** inverts the Christian tradition of the righteous being admitted to paradise by the saints and angels at the Pearly Gates. The monumental scale of the vast ruin gives the impression of a once colossal power and evokes resonances of supernatural fears. The castle, isolated, inaccessible and inhospitable, with 'frowning walls and dark window openings', is a secluded place of danger. It is a thing of a mysterious past and not part of the modern world that Harker so innocently represents.

Count Dracula has the most marvellously theatrical villain's entrance. Jonathan hears the heavy footsteps approaching; the door is unfastened with rattling of chains, clanking of bolts and grating

CHECK THE FILM

Max Schreck was a memorable pale and thin vampire in *Nosferatu* (1922), with his shaven scalp, sunken cheeks, bulging eyes and fingernails like claws. In the 1931 film *Dracula* the Hungarian Bela Lugosi, with his heavy, authentic accent, pinched lips, deathly complexion and dark, severe features, captured popular imagination.

CONTEXT

The eighteenth-century Swiss theologian and poet, Johann Kaspar Lavater, believed that there was a connection between facial traits and character. In his *Essays on Physiognomy and One Hundred Physiognomical Rules*, Lavater offered such advice as 'the more the chin, the more the man' and 'as are the lips so is the character'.

noises. Stoker does not prolong our moment of suspense here as the door swings back to reveal a 'tall old man' (p. 15). Although he is tall, clean-shaven and courtly, Dracula is 'without a single speck of colour about him anywhere'. This is an indicator of his nature, his lack of true vitality. He is dressed entirely in black, symbolic of death and mourning.

Jonathan notes Dracula's striking intonation and strength, observing that his host's hand is 'more like the hand of a dead than a living man'. Dracula's dialogue is overtly archaic, almost ceremonial in the formality of his greeting. Stoker here simulates the exactitude of expression that an old aristocrat might be expected to adopt with an unfamiliar language, or a language that is known only through reading rather than through conversation. His command of the English language is, as is revealed later, based on a formal and literary turn of phrase from his study of books. This creates an unsettling contrast between the literal meaning of his words and their effect. The invitation to 'Enter freely and of your own will!' seems more an equivocal warning than a warm welcome (p. 15).

Jonathan finds Count Dracula 'courteous' and 'graceful' (p. 16), impressions that confirm the description given by Harker's employer Hawkins of the young solicitor's 'very faithful disposition'. Jonathan trusts and expects an aristocrat to have such qualities and is not surprised by oddities of local custom. He reflects on Count Dracula's 'physiognomy', alluding here to the ancient view that character is revealed through physical features denoting certain human qualities. Dracula's face is 'a strong – very strong – aquiline, with high bridge of the thin nose and … with lofty domed forehead', these being traits associated with power and intellect (p. 16). Dracula is a bundle of strange and contradictory qualities; but his unhealthy nature is confirmed in Harker's physical reaction to being touched by him.

Count Dracula's comments on the howling of the wolves – 'the children of the night. What music they make!' – serve to define the relationship between Jonathan and his host: 'you dwellers in the city cannot enter into the feelings of the hunter' (p. 17).

The remark, taken literally, is merely an offhand pleasantry acknowledging the difference between the modern, urban life and the traditional, dangerous life in a wild country. But Dracula understands the music and the feelings of the wolves because he is also a hunter. This remark also implies Dracula's connection to the wolves and hints at his dominant role in that they are 'children'. Dracula's comment, taken in this light, shows a predator's cruel contempt for his prey.

There is a remarkable tension underlying the encounters between the Count and Jonathan, which is the source of the latter's growing unease and fear. The Englishman is part of Dracula's study and preparation for entering the modern world, to be dispensed with thereafter. Jonathan is as yet unaware of the threat and takes the Count on trust. Yet, as the incident with the mirror shows, Count Dracula finds it difficult to control his own bloodlust. It is the repressed urge that fuels the suspense at this point. How long will the Count play this game of deception? When will Jonathan realise what is going on?

There is a curious blurring of the relationship here. Dracula is the host and Jonathan the guest, yet, as Dracula's agent, Jonathan must follow the Count's instructions. A professional solicitor is far from a servant or slave, but the imperious nature of the Count, as an aristocrat and the Englishman's social superior, puts Jonathan at a disadvantage when later his fears become more pressing. A protracted game of double bluff then develops, where neither Harker nor Dracula openly acknowledges the truth of the situation.

Dracula's aristocratic nature is highlighted in their discussion of the blue flames and the buried treasure; he sees the peasants as cowardly and foolish. In this attitude he is perhaps more honest than Jonathan, whose own recorded views tend to be more patronising. The Count has all the certainty of his own nobility and, as he says, he is accustomed to being the master. He obviously realises that being 'a stranger in a strange land' may jeopardise his freedom to act as the master (p. 19). It is clear there are limits to his power, and that Dracula wishes to grow beyond those limits. He resembles a caged beast waiting for the moment of escape.

CONTEXT

Boundaries are both physical and mental constructions, and the people who cross them are explorers and adventurers. There are always consequences for going beyond the limits, whether they are social or personal. Fear of those consequences is a powerful social inhibition which prevents most people from straying too far.

CONTEXT

Photography had been in development since 1826. Kodak, a word without particular meaning, was a trade name invented by George Eastman, the company's founder.

CONTEXT

The word 'saturnine' means dark and gloomy, and is derived from the god of agriculture, whose name, Saturn, was given by ancient astrologers to the most remote planet they knew. It also comes from the word ancient alchemists used for lead.

GLOSSARY

31 **culverin** a large, long and thin cannon

31 **fastnesses** strongholds or easily defended positions

34 **ribald** derived from the ancient Germanic word for 'whore', and words used for menial servants in feudal times, this suggests debauched or crude sexual behaviour

34 **coquetry** flirtatiousness

Jonathan Harker uses modern technology ('Kodak' was an early synonym for the camera) to introduce Carfax, another Gothic ruin, resembling a dilapidated fortress with its barred gates and windows. He describes Dracula's 'malignant' and 'saturnine' expression as he speaks of his preference for life in the shadows (p. 22). Jonathan, despite his interest in physiognomy, does not understand that the cold, cruel and infectious evil he glimpses in Dracula's smile is more than 'his cast of face'.

Stoker, in this chapter, has done much of the work in establishing the facets of Count Dracula's character, particularly his nocturnal nature. He casts no reflection. The demon within him is brought to the surface by the sight of Harker's blood and subdued by the symbol of Christianity. There are many possible interpretations of the vampire and what he represents, but there is clearly a sensual energy to this character that alarms and threatens Harker's orderly and commonplace beliefs. Jonathan's realisation that he is a prisoner is heightened by the description of the beautiful view from his window, underlining the fact that he is now cut off from the natural world.

CHAPTER 3

- Jonathan is impressed by Count Dracula's intimate knowledge of local history and his grasp of legal detail.
- He witnesses Dracula's departures from the castle.
- Jonathan is visited by three women, who are restrained by the Count.
- He realises he is to be a victim of these women at Count Dracula's pleasure.

Jonathan realises he cannot risk acknowledging his situation by confronting the Count. When he sees the Count making his bed, he realises there are no servants in the Castle and that the coach driver must also have been the Count. Jonathan remembers, with a fright, how the driver had commanded the wolves. He decides to find out more about the Count, in order to understand his predicament.

Count Dracula speaks of the history of Transylvania as if he had been present at all the battles he describes. He clearly holds the contemporary aristocracy in contempt as he speaks of a warlike past. Dracula claims descent from Attila, the notorious warlord.

Jonathan is impressed by Count Dracula's knowledge of legal and administrative affairs and he is questioned closely on points that will have a bearing on Dracula's future movements. The Count asks him to write some letters announcing a delay in his return to England. He warns Harker never to fall asleep in any room of the castle except his bedroom as this will lead to bad dreams and other unspoken consequences.

Jonathan describes with horror how he witnesses the Count slithering lizard-like down the wall of the castle. The second time this happens, he takes the opportunity to explore. He discovers another part of the castle, furnished more comfortably than his own rooms. Having finished writing in his diary, he falls asleep.

Recalling what happens next, Harker once more finds it hard to know whether he was asleep and dreaming or awake and experiencing something real. He hopes it was only a dream but fears it was real. Three young ladies visit him by moonlight. They are similar in appearance to the Count and cast no shadow. He describes their 'voluptuous lips' and his longing to be kissed by them (p. 33). One of the women approaches Harker, and her sharp teeth are just making contact with his neck when the Count intervenes.

The Count promises the women they shall have Harker when he has finished with him. He throws them a bag containing a child, which they take as they disappear.

COMMENTARY

Stoker constructs an extraordinary sequence of events in this chapter, extending Harker's participation in the Count's masquerade of normality and sustaining the suspense over a bloodthirsty recitation of the Dracula family history. The sequence

CONTEXT

Attila the Hun (c.406–53) was known as the Scourge of God. King of the Huns, his rule extended over Germany and Scythia from the Rhine to the borders of China. In 447 he devastated all the lands between the Mediterranean and the Black Sea.

CONTEXT

'Voluptuous' suggests sensuous pleasures and self-indulgence, associated in the nineteenth century with a fuller-figured ideal form of feminine beauty.

CONTEXT
In Greek mythology sirens were women or winged creatures whose sweet singing lured unwary sailors onto rocks. In Homer's epic poem the *Odyssey*, Odysseus ordered his men to block their ears with wax and tied himself to the mast of his ship to escape their songs as they sailed past. The word later became used to mean a dangerous, alluring woman.

concludes with a brief respite for Jonathan that immediately leads to the sudden introduction of a new threat in the form of the young women who, like the sirens in ancient mythology, wish to lead him to his doom.

The sensual description of Jonathan's perilous encounter with these vampires has been described by some as erotic, even pornographic, though the passage may seem tame by the more explicit standards of early twenty-first-century fiction. The startling combination of the sexual urge with both pleasurable submission and the threat of death, in very animalistic terms, is still one of the more memorable moments in the novel. This is partly achieved simply by the **narrative perspective** being that of the willing victim and partly by the swift development of this episode in contrast to the slow build-up that precedes it. It is also the enactment of a typical male sexual fantasy in which three beautiful women dominate one man.

The power of the crucifix is quickly glossed over as Jonathan tries to make sense of his plight. He accepts it in a pragmatic rather than religious way and postpones making his mind up about the matter. His scepticism is representative of the self-consciously scientific outlook of the Victorian era which Stoker seems to take some delight in mocking.

Jonathan, despite his fears and suspicions, finds the Count's history and the manner in which it is related quite fascinating. This fits well with his character, as delineated in the earlier chapters, being interested in historical detail. This gives Stoker an opportunity to provide the background to the origins of the vampire, in an indirect manner that is opaque to Harker but discernible to the reader. He adds, with a rhetorical flourish, werewolves, witches and devils to the mix of warlike tribes, Norse gods and marauding invaders. There is a hint of a treacherous past contained in this speech alongside the fiercely acclaimed despotism. Dracula clearly reveres the political notion of strong leadership and shows neither remorse nor pity for the people that fell in battle.

Dracula denounces the Hapsburgs and Romanoffs, then the most powerful dynasties in Europe, as 'mushroom growths' in comparison to his family. His remark 'Blood is too precious a thing in these days of dishonourable peace' has a fatal, almost prophetic, resonance (p. 26). Within twenty years of this novel's publication, the Hapsburg and the Romanoff dynasties collapsed in the war that consumed the lives of many thousands of their subjects.

Dracula's dominance over Harker is confirmed in the latter's acceptance of the instruction to write letters explaining his delayed departure. Both characters are aware of each other's understanding of the situation yet they continue the pretence that this is a normal business transaction between solicitor and client.

Jonathan describes briefly the sight of Dracula's exit from the window before his narrative is interrupted for three days. It appears he is too terrified at this point to continue with his journal. When the narrative resumes, there is a more urgent note of determination in his writing as he formulates a plan of escape. His excursions into unknown parts of the castle bring him little comfort, and despite his delight in modern technology (in the form of shorthand writing) he cannot shake the loneliness that his ancient surroundings enforce upon him.

Harker's encounter with the vampire women is one of the most obviously sexualised parts of the narrative. His response to their approach brings him a sense of shame, betrayal and humiliation. He is drawn to their animal natures ('I closed my eyes in a languorous ecstasy and waited – waited with beating heart') but reprieved by his captor. He takes refuge, in his writing, from the uncertain fear that his experience may have been more than imaginary.

The Count and his vampires clash in a reproachful and hostile exchange. Stoker's dialogue for the women's protest to Dracula, 'You yourself never loved; you never love!', manages to convey a weird ambiguity (p. 34). Is it a flirtatious challenge, an expression of predatory hunger for blood, sheer sexual frustration or, perhaps, a yearning for something more emotional? Dracula reminds them that love, whatever it might have been, is a thing of their past: 'Yes, I too can love; you yourselves can tell it from the past.' It is here that we

---

CONTEXT

Blood has a literal as well as **metaphorical** significance in Victorian times. The notion of the bloodline of a family or a race as something to be preserved at all costs was the basis for the exclusivity of class and national identity.

CONTEXT

The adjective 'languorous' used here by Jonathan Harker (p. 34) comes from the noun 'languor', which can be used to mean a heavy mood of depression associated with sorrow, sexual frustration or, more poetically, unrequited love.

CHECK THE FILM
The eroticism of the female vampire is central to Tony Scott's *The Hunger* (1983), with fine performances from David Bowie, Catherine Deneuve and Susan Sarandon.

GLOSSARY

35 **suavest** the most polite or agreeable personal manner or charm

38 **mattock** ancient agricultural tool, rather like a pickaxe, used for digging

40 **thrall** to be held as a slave or captive

40 **vaporous garment** insubstantial or flimsy material, rather suggestive of see-through lingerie, though the overt meaning is a reference to Harker's true courage emerging

have a sense, perhaps, of a fleeting moment in which we might pity these creatures who have outlived the memory of love. But Stoker swiftly dashes this embryonic sentiment, the women hungrily disappearing with a child to devour.

Jonathan, overcome with horror, knowing he is promised to the women, passes out. It is a theatrical climax, a 'blackout', that brings the curtain down swiftly on the release of the tension so carefully built and sustained.

See **Text 1** of **Extended commentaries** for further discussion of part of this chapter.

CHAPTER 4

- Jonathan Harker's attempt to smuggle a message out of the castle is betrayed.
- He discovers Count Dracula sleeping in a box in the ruined chapel.
- Count Dracula's journey to London begins.
- Jonathan makes a desperate escape by climbing down the sheer cliff face.

Jonathan Harker wakes up in his room and realises that he is only temporarily safe from the women who are waiting to suck his blood. He accepts that he was not dreaming. Count Dracula insists he writes three letters for dated dispatch over the next month. Harker deduces from this how little time he has left to live.

Jonathan attempts to smuggle some letters out by bribing some of the gypsies who visit the castle. Count Dracula shows him he has intercepted these and destroys the shorthand note to Mina. Harker's personal effects and clothing are removed from his room; it seems there is no escape.

After a gap of two weeks, Jonathan resumes the journal. Some more peasants arrive at the castle delivering large empty boxes, but his appeals to them are thwarted again by the gypsies loyal to Dracula, the Szgany. Count Dracula goes out hunting again dressed in the clothes stolen from Jonathan, and he realises Dracula is using him as a cover for his hunting and also preparing a false trail to cover the Englishman's disappearance. Harker sees phantom shapes appearing and retreats to his room; sometime later he hears dreadful sounds from the Count's room.

A peasant woman arrives, sees Jonathan at the window and demands that he return her child. As she beats at the door of the castle, Jonathan hears the Count calling to the wolves. He does not pity her fate.

Now Harker takes decisive action. He prepares to climb down the sheer face of the castle wall to enter the Count's room; he writes a farewell to Mina in his journal, knowing that he is risking his life. Dracula's room is filled with piles of old gold. Jonathan explores the ruined chapel and graveyard, and discovers Dracula sleeping as if dead in one of fifty boxes of earth. He sees a frightening look of hatred in Dracula's stony eyes.

Some four days later, Harker again sees Count Dracula masquerading in his stolen clothes, and demands to be allowed to leave. The Count opens the door and Jonathan is faced with a pack of wolves. Dracula's cruelty is apparent in his enjoyment of this moment.

Harker hears Dracula restraining the three women once more. He knows he has run out of time, and falls to the ground in prayer. In the morning, Jonathan climbs down the wall again to Dracula's lair, searching for a key to the door. He sees Dracula again in the chapel, but the Count is now rejuvenated: 'gorged with blood; he lay like a filthy leech, exhausted with his repletion' (p. 44). He describes the 'gouts of fresh blood' trickling over his lips and chin. Jonathan contemplates the horrific prospect of Dracula in London and realises he has been instrumental in enabling the

 CHECK THE FILM

In Joel Schumacher's 1997 film *The Lost Boys*, starring Kiefer Sutherland, a young boy joins with two vampire hunters in an attempt to save his elder brother from the curse of vampirism by hunting down and destroying the head vampire.

CHECK THE FILM

Tod Browning's *Dracula* (1931) was an adaptation of Hamilton Deane and John Balderston's successful play *Dracula: The Vampire Play*. Bela Lugosi as Count Dracula, who had already created this role on stage, established the image on screen that has been so culturally influential. He was only given the part after Lon Chaney, star of other horror films, was unable to take it. This is also the first horror film with recorded sound.

monster to invade England. He grabs a shovel and leaps to the attack but is paralysed by the sight of the Count turning to stare at him. Harker returns to Dracula's room as the Szgany remove the boxes in the chapel.

Dracula has left the castle. Jonathan, now alone with the three women, knows there is no more time. He takes some of Dracula's gold and prepares to risk the precipice rather than face the women. His journal concludes with a farewell to his fiancée, Mina.

COMMENTARY

This chapter begins with Jonathan Harker convincing himself of the reality of his experiences with the three women and takes him further into the depths of despair as he encounters Dracula in his horrid lair.

The façade of normality the two characters maintain is threatened by Harker's attempts to communicate with, or escape to, the world beyond the castle, but the pretence is never abandoned. The Count clearly has the upper hand throughout. He taunts Harker over the letter coded in shorthand ('a vile thing, an outrage upon friendship and hospitality') but obligingly forwards the open and unthreatening letter to Hawkins, Harker's employer, apologising for opening it by mistake: 'Your letters are sacred to me. Your pardon, my friend, that unknowingly I did break the seal' (p. 37). This is a menacing display of power which underlines how Harker is now truly isolated.

The second duel of wits between the two characters is Harker's last attempt to challenge Dracula. Jonathan is surprised by Dracula's courteous acceptance of his wish to depart immediately, yet there is no real possibility of his leaving the castle. Effectively, Dracula is inviting him to choose between being devoured by the wolves now or by the women a little later on. Stoker invests his character with a ghoulish delight in tormenting the unfortunate Harker, who notes the Count's 'red light of triumph in his eyes' and his smile 'that Judas in hell might be proud of' (p. 43).

The Count's control over the wolves is confirmed emphatically through the obscene slaughter of the mother of the abducted child. This passage constructs our understanding of the vampires as evil beyond redemption. They are monsters that prey on children without remorse. The destruction of mother and child here is emblematic of the terror that Dracula represents to Stoker's society.

Jonathan, in his prison, is mistakenly accused by the mother, as Dracula intended. His lack of pity for her death strikes a discordant note and marks possibly the lowest point of his desperation: 'I could not pity her, for I knew now what had become of her child, and she was better dead' (p. 40). Stoker has interwoven the incidents here of the vampires' second approach to Jonathan, the death of the child and the death of the mother to intensify the horror of his imprisonment and impending doom.

He narrowly escapes being hypnotised by the women as they approach him a second time. It is not entirely clear whether he is saved from them or from his own desires when he runs away screaming. This is the first explicit mention of hypnotism in the novel, though by no means the last.

Stoker has Jonathan Harker visit Dracula in his box twice. Harker has been brave enough to climb down a sheer wall to explore the castle in search of an escape route. His second adventure is the more daunting because he knows what he must face in order to secure his safety. He suggests that he is no match for Dracula's hypnotic powers when he describes the 'basilisk horror' of the dead eyes glaring at him (p. 45). Stoker does not need to emphasise the point, as the notion of hypnotic, telepathic or supernatural power is now well established in the narrative. If Jonathan fears being hypnotised by the women, it seems obvious that Dracula is an even greater threat to the independence of his mind. That the Count can exert this influence even when at rest makes him an almost invincible nemesis, and Stoker shows us Harker seemingly unable to harm Dracula. In fact, as is revealed later, he has placed his mark on Dracula and this foreshadows the final, inevitable conflict. It shows Dracula is indeed powerful, but not invulnerable. Harker is forced to flee, conscious only of his failure to destroy the monster.

CONTEXT

The Victorian age publicly idealised the innocence of childhood and the sanctity of motherhood. This was partly related to the high infant mortality rate and uncertain risks of childbirth for women. In comparison to the reality of existence for the majority of women and children at the end of the nineteenth century, such views may seem sentimental and indulgent.

CONTEXT

A basilisk, the king of serpents, reputedly has a deadly stare: to look into this creature's eyes is instantly fatal. Also known as a cockatrice, and supposedly hatched by a snake from a cock's egg, this fearsome mythical creature has featured in many stories since it was first described by the Roman author Pliny in AD77.

CHECK THE BOOK

The identification of sleep and death has a long literary history. Shakespeare's *Hamlet*, already mentioned by Stoker in Chapter 3, has the most well-known contemplation of mortality in our theatrical heritage: 'To be, or not to be, that is the question ...' (*Hamlet*, III.1.56–69).

The pace of events moves quickly from this point to the conclusion of this first part of the novel. Jonathan hears Dracula being carried out of the castle by the gypsies. Again the perspective of the narrative emphasises his isolation all the more now that he is trapped in Dracula's room. As he prepares to climb down, he envisages his death at the foot of the castle wall as a welcome and peaceful sleep: 'At least God's mercy is better than that of these monsters, and the precipice is steep and high. At its foot a man may sleep – as a man' (p. 46). Hypnotism is derived from the name of the Greek god of sleep, Hypnos. Stoker's motif of sleep and sleeplessness expands to convey notions of the real and unreal, sexual desire and perversion, death and afterlife, dreams and nightmares.

The last word of the chapter is his despairing call of his fiancée's name: 'Mina!' This is not the first time he ends his journal entry in this fashion, but now it acts as the cue for Mina Murray to take over the narration. This rather theatrical link is a quite obvious device to herald the introduction of a new voice. Stoker is experimenting, exploiting the shifting differences between the appearance of things and their reality.

CHAPTER 5

- Mina Murray looks forward to her fiancé's return from abroad.
- Her friend Lucy Westenra receives three marriage proposals.
- Lucy chooses to accept Arthur Holmwood's proposal.
- Quincey Morris and Dr John Seward, both unlucky in love, maintain their friendship with Arthur.

Mina Murray apologises, in a brief letter, to her old friend Lucy Westenra. Mina's work as a schoolmistress leaves her little time for writing. She explains how interested she is in a variety of forms of writing and how she intends to keep a diary, trying to work like 'lady journalists', accurately recording all she sees and hears (p. 46).

GLOSSARY

51 Kingdom Come a form of the Christian expression for the day when God will establish a kingdom on earth; a **metaphor** for the end of time or 'for ever'

53 the Korea an old way of referring to the Korean peninsula, scene of a number of American military adventures in pursuit of influence over trade and economic development during the nineteenth century

She anticipates with excitement the return of her fiancé, Jonathan Harker. She asks for Lucy's news and suggests she has heard rumours of romantic interest.

Lucy Westenra replies to Mina's letter, at first denying there is any news to share, then confessing her secret love for someone. She refers to two men in the letter: Mr Holmwood, who is mentioned as if in passing, and an unnamed doctor, who is given much more attention. It is not immediately obvious for which gentleman she is declaring her love.

Lucy writes to Mina, again in reply (to a letter not contained in the narrative), thanking her for her sympathetic response. She relates the extraordinary sequence of marriage proposals she has just experienced. The report of the first proposal from Dr John Seward is not fully detailed. The second scene, of Quincey P. Morris's proposal, is related with more warmth, and the unusual nature of his manner of speech ('American slang') is vividly captured in the excerpts from their dialogue quoted by Lucy (p. 50). The third proposal, from Arthur Holmwood, is related with the least detail of all. Her description of the moment recalls the old saying: 'Actions speak louder than words.' Lucy is clearly delighted with the outcome and she implies that she has told Arthur all her secrets.

Dr John Seward, known to his friends as Jack, records his personal diary using a phonograph. As he speaks, noting the month incorrectly, he briefly mentions his 'rebuff' by Lucy and then considers how he must seek a cure for his own unhappiness in his work with his patients. He makes a range of comments on his most fascinating patient, R. M. Renfield. He records his view that Renfield is 'a possibly dangerous man' (p. 52).

Quincey P. Morris writes a friendly letter to Arthur Holmwood, reminding him of their shared experiences as friends and inviting Arthur to celebrate his engagement with his less fortunate rivals. Quincey promises that he and Dr Seward will give Arthur a 'hearty welcome and a loving greeting' (p. 53). Arthur Holmwood sends a

CHECK THE BOOK

In 'The Canterville Ghost' (serialised in the *Court and Society Review* in 1887) Oscar Wilde wrote: 'we have really everything in common with America nowadays, except, of course, language'.

CONTEXT

The phonograph is a sound recording device invented by the American Thomas Edison in 1877.

telegram, two sentences long, agreeing to the celebrations and suggesting he will share with them his knowledge of Lucy's feelings.

COMMENTARY

This chapter, the shortest in the novel, briskly establishes five new characters in striking contrast to one another using a variety of narrative devices. We move – without warning – from the one narrator's voice that has held our attention over the previous four chapters to the interplay of fragmented, multiple **narrative perspectives** given in swift succession over six pages or so.

The **tone** of the novel is abruptly changed at this point. Jonathan Harker, poised, at the end of the fourth chapter, on the edge of a 'steep and high' precipice (risking death in his attempt to escape the ruined castle and the clutches of the vampire women) remains in this 'cliffhanger' position until he re-enters the narrative three chapters further on. The Gothic **melodrama** of his journal is relieved by the gossip and flirtation of the two young women's exchange of letters. The excitement of Lucy Westenra's romantic dilemma is followed by the steady manner of Dr Seward's stoical recording; the rough and ready companionship of Quincey Morris's letter of invitation; and the more upbeat, if rather smug, amusement of Arthur Holmwood's telegram.

The two women reveal themselves to be of rather different character. Mina Murray is employed, seeking self-improvement and dedicated to perfecting secretarial skills to assist her future husband: 'if I can stenograph well enough I can take down what he wants to say' (p. 48). Her comment 'It must be so nice to see strange countries' is **ironic** evidence of her naivety, given the perils currently threatening her fiancé (p. 47). Lucy Westenra, on the other hand, is leading a comfortable existence of leisure at home, and she clearly enjoys the fact that she is pursued by numerous wealthy and attractive young men. There is an **ambivalence** in her attitude that hints at a self-indulgent, possibly even promiscuous, nature. She scolds herself for being 'a horrid flirt' (p. 50). When she admits she must try not to be ungrateful that she has been sent 'such a lover, such a husband, and such a friend' (p. 52), it is not clear whether she is referring to one man or to all three men in whichever order.

CONTEXT
Mina Murray's account begins around the time that Jonathan Harker realises he is a captive in Castle Dracula.

CONTEXT
Stenography is the act of writing notes in shorthand, a skill that was becoming widely used in the nineteenth century.

The three men, who will become the heroes of the quest to defeat Dracula, are set out as quite different types. Dr John Seward is depicted by Lucy, and by himself, to be reserved emotionally and very much the rational thinking man of science. Quincey P. Morris is, with far greater sentimental awareness, a frontiersman of the New World, an adventurer and a man of action, whose tales make Lucy 'sympathise with poor Desdemona when she had such a dangerous stream poured in her ear' (p. 49).

Arthur Holmwood is more indirectly revealed by Lucy's comments. He is no match for Morris in his story-telling abilities or his ability to create opportunities to be alone with Lucy. Her attentive description of Dr Seward's physical attractions and her omission of the detail of Arthur's appearance suggest he may not be the most handsome of the three men. Lucy's offhand comment that 'he and mamma get on very well together' suggests there is parental approval for her choice of husband (p. 47). She has made a good match. Arthur will later inherit a noble title and, as such, is a man of influence, a 'noble man'.

Quincey Morris's invitation unites the men and reasserts their past bonds of friendship. Their shared adventures have taken them across the globe and this not only hints at their abilities and courage but defines them as men of the world in contrast to the women, who are allowed to be partially active only in the fields of domesticity, culture and education.

> **CONTEXT**
>
> Desdemona is the heroine of Shakespeare's tragedy *Othello*, attracted to the war hero Othello, who kills her in a jealous passion. Lucy is referring to the attractions of risk and danger, indicating again the unwise, wilder part of her nature.

CHAPTER 6

- Mina Murray arrives in Whitby.
- Lucy Westenra develops a strange habit of sleepwalking.
- Dr Seward learns about his patient Renfield's unusual diet.
- An old man, Mr Swales, talks of lies, suicide and approaching death.

GLOSSARY

GLOSSARY

56 Day of Judgment Islam, Judaism and Christianity have related but separate concepts of divine retribution for human error

59 carrion meat unfit for human consumption, often verminous or rotting flesh

60 zoophagous adjective describing someone or something which feeds on animals or living flesh

60 vivisection surgical experimentation on living animals, particularly controversial in the latter part of the twentieth century

CONTEXT

To disgorge something means to vomit, though with a sense of expelling something that should not have been swallowed, as in the biblical tale of Jonah being swallowed by the whale and being heaved out of its mouth.

It is now August. Mina Murray visits her friend Lucy Westenra in Whitby. She is drawn to a seat in the graveyard above the town that gives a fine view over the sea. Lucy accompanies her and they meet and talk with three old men. One of the old men, Mr Swales, is dismissive when Mina mentions the legends of ghosts in the ruined abbey. The harbour of Whitby is described and legends of ships lost at sea are mentioned. Mr Swales speaks disparagingly about the influence of such scary stories, and goes on to denounce the lies cut into the tombstones in the graveyard. Lucy is dismayed to learn that their favourite seat overlooks the misrepresented grave of a suicide. Mr Swales points out there is nothing to fear from the dead.

Lucy is looking forward to her wedding to Arthur Holmwood. Talk of the marriage makes Mina lonely as she has had no news of her fiancé, Jonathan Harker, for a month.

Dr Seward records in his diary his case notes on the patient Renfield. Renfield catches flies and eats them. He feeds the flies to spiders; he eats the spiders. He feeds the spiders to birds; he eats the birds (an attendant informs Seward that Renfield 'has disgorged a whole lot of feathers'). He requests a kitten, but Dr Seward is growing concerned, and defines Renfield as a 'zoophagous (life-eating) maniac' (p. 60). Renfield keeps an account of the lives consumed in a little notebook. Dr Seward comments in his diary on his feelings for Lucy and complains of lack of motivation in his work.

Mina writes in shorthand of troubling circumstances. She is concerned for Jonathan's absence; and now Lucy seems to have taken to sleepwalking, alarming her mother, Mrs Westenra. Both Mina and Lucy have difficulty sleeping.

A storm is approaching Whitby. Mr Swales talks to Mina, apologising for his attitude, and speaks about his acceptance of his imminent death. A ship that does not seem to be under anyone's control is seen approaching.

COMMENTARY

Stoker's detailed research in preparing this novel is particularly evident in this chapter. It is still possible to visit the harbour of Whitby and see the places he describes so accurately here. But Stoker does not dwell too much on descriptive detail. The plot develops apace as the narrative burden of the chapter is shuttled between two **narrators**. The sequence of events and timing is not entirely chronological here, and the leaps backward and forward in time are disconcerting.

Mr Swales, at first, is an irreverent old cynic who is openly hostile to what he perceives to be the hypocrisy of the Church and superstition of the people. Stoker makes this character speak in a form of 'Whitby vernacular', and the old man has the forthrightness of expression often associated with stereotypes of working-class people from the north of England. Mr Swales enjoys making rude remarks about Lucy sitting on a dead man's lap to tease the young women, though there is a gruesome and prophetic undertone beneath Stoker's humour. The women keep their seat and enjoy the beauty of the view, but their favourite place is not what they thought it was. It will become a crucial point of intersection in the plot as the grave is, according to tradition, made unholy by the burial of a suicide. It is no comfort either that the suicide and his family were of bad character.

Mina closes her entry on a note of isolation and loneliness. We are reminded of Jonathan Harker's journal, though her **tone** is one of solitary concern rather than anxious desperation. She is detached from the society around her with its competing influences of dance music and psalm singing by the Salvation Army. Stoker neatly encapsulates this character's balanced moral outlook in Mina's recognition that neither band is aware of the other's music, yet she can hear both. Mina can appreciate the lively and delightful along with the dour and dutiful. This is why she is able to be a friend and mentor to Lucy, who has less stability in her nature.

CONTEXT

Whitby, in Yorkshire, had a history as a whaling port. It was well known as the place where Captain Cook began his voyages of exploration that contributed to the development of the British Empire. Following the success of *Dracula*, the village has attracted many visitors on account of its connection with Stoker's famous vampire; and there is even a Whitby Dracula Society.

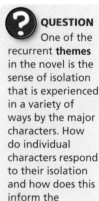

QUESTION One of the recurrent **themes** in the novel is the sense of isolation that is experienced in a variety of ways by the major characters. How do individual characters respond to their isolation and how does this inform the reader's attitude to each character?

Stoker leaps back in time to follow the development of the madness in Renfield before returning to focus on Lucy. Dr Seward's diary shows him to be ambitious for success in his profession, but rather sadly at a loss now that his love for Lucy is unrequited. Renfield's mad appetites fascinate him but are also repulsive. He wants to advance human understanding of the brain but lacks 'sufficient cause' (p. 60): he feels that Renfield is more motivated and dedicated to pursuing his zoophagous mania than he himself is to his work.

Seward's lament for the girl he has lost leads the narrative back to Mina's concerns about Lucy and her sleepwalking. Stoker has woven some more intricate threads of loss, love, madness and motivation into his motif of sleeplessness. He makes this sleeping disorder a trait of his more wilful character, Lucy Westenra. It is a trait inherited from her father, possibly suggesting a masculine sense of independence, but also a revival of an old habit, which confirms her immaturity. Lucy is a 'wild child' in many ways. The threat of the approaching storm seems to disturb her.

Mr Swales is given the opportunity to mend his irreligious ways by apologising to Mina for his habitual joking about death. He explains to her, in a speech that uses fewer dialect expressions, that he is old and knows he must die soon. Being afraid of death, he has taken to joking about it as a defence. His last speech is not as reassuring as he seems to intend. He speaks of 'something in that wind … that sounds, and looks, and tastes, and smells like death. It's in the air' (p. 63). Death is something tangible to Mr Swales. Stoker shows this disreputable character to be a devout and faithful person, moved to prayer by the atmosphere that precedes the storm.

Stoker uses a minor character to pass the baton of the narrative as the chapter is drawn to a close. A coastguard sets up the next link to the following chapter about the foreign ship: 'We'll hear more of her' (p. 64).

CONTEXT

In the early nineteenth century, somnambulism was a popular theme in theatre and literature, inspired by the early psychological investigations by scientists who believed that sleepwalking was a direct link between dreaming and madness.

CHAPTER 7

- A ship, with a dead man at the helm, arrives in the harbour at Whitby.
- Count Dracula's boxes are unloaded.
- The captain's log recounts a tale of horror at sea.
- Mr Swales is found dead at Mina and Lucy's favourite seat overlooking the graveyard.

The chapter opens with a newspaper correspondent reporting on the calm before the storm, the sudden onset of a great tempest, and the drama of a near disaster at sea. This sequence of events introduces the main report on the arrival of an unmanned ship in Whitby harbour during the night. A large dog leaps off the ship and disappears into the dark graveyard.

The captain of the ship is discovered tied to the ship's wheel with a crucifix in his hand. He has been dead for two days. There are some legal matters to settle regarding the ownership of the vessel and its cargo. Count Dracula's boxes are delivered ashore; and a local dog is discovered dead, its body terribly mutilated.

The ship's captain kept a record of events in Russian which is translated for the reporter. The captain's log records the gradual disappearance of his crew and their fears of a stranger on board. His last crewman chooses to drown rather than face the 'fiend or monster' (p. 72). The captain is left to face his death alone. The investigation of the deaths of the crew members concludes with an 'open' verdict. This 'mystery of the sea' is thought to be the work of a maniac, possibly the captain himself (p. 73).

Mina Murray cannot sleep through the storm. Lucy Westenra twice gets up and puts on clothes without waking up, but returns to bed when Mina interrupts her. Mina is still concerned about Jonathan Harker.

GLOSSARY

69 rescript although this had a particular legal and religious meaning in earlier times, here it refers to a duplicate or second draft form of writing

74 agglomeration bundle of things gathered together; sometimes used in nineteenth-century studies of volcanic matter, so suggesting the fusing together of separate things into an inseparable mass

 CHECK THE NET
Dracula travels aboard the *Demeter*. The ship is named after the Greek goddess of fertility. You can find out more about her by searching the Encyclopedia Mythica website at **www.pantheon.org**

At the funeral of the sea captain, Lucy is restless and ill at ease. Mr Swales is found dead at their favourite seat in the graveyard, and a dog shows fear at the tombstone of the suicide's grave. Mina is worried that these strange events will further disturb Lucy. She takes Lucy for a long walk to try to make her tired enough to sleep more easily.

COMMENTARY

The byline 'From a correspondent' was commonly attached to newspaper articles in the Victorian era to mask the identity of the writer and could be variously understood to suggest, for example, that the writer was an aspiring amateur journalist, or a well-informed but secret source of information, or a person without sufficient reputation to warrant their name being added to the report. While it is true that not all journalists were credited, the lack of gender identity was also an editorial device to avoid offending the readership.

CHECK THE BOOK

A detailed and informative account of the experience of 'lady journalists', women as professional writers, can be found in Barbara Onslow's *Women of the Press in Nineteenth-Century Britain* (2000).

We may wonder whether 'a Correspondent' (p. 64) is, in fact, Mina Murray fulfilling her ambition to become a 'lady journalist'. The language of the article is similar in **tone** and expression to Mina's journal and quite unlike the voice of the only other example of newspaper journalism incorporated in the narrative (Chapter 11). Such an assumption has to remain as speculation on our part, however, since it is never stated by Stoker that Mina is the author of this article.

The account of the sunset in advance of the storm is a particularly colourful passage of descriptive writing, the 'downward way' of the sun 'marked by myriad clouds of every sunset-colour – flame, purple, pink, green, violet, and all the tints of gold' (p. 64). It is a vivid and heated contrast with the dull greyness that dominated Mina's reflections towards the end of the preceding chapter ('Everything is grey … grey earthy rock, grey clouds … grey sea, into which the sand-points stretch like grey fingers', p. 62).

Stoker does not rush headlong into the arrival of the Russian ship. The gathering storm is a major event for Whitby, and there is a sense of excitement for those witnessing the power of the weather. There are spectators and participants in the drama of the tempest, and a massive searchlight illuminates the harbour from the cliffs above, picking out the 'corpse, with drooping head', at the helm (p. 67). Our sense of anticipation is heightened as we expect Count Dracula to return to the foreground of the narrative. We know what cargo is on the ship and we connect the restlessness of Lucy, the morbid fascination of Mr Swales and the storm itself to the imminence of Dracula's arrival.

Stoker here leaves us to imagine the ability of Dracula to control the weather; it needs no elaboration. The narrative now operates almost entirely through the **ironic** mode. The author has skewed the relationship between the text and the reader so that we are aware we are picking up meanings that are entirely hidden from the **narrator**.

Dracula now leaps ashore in the form of an 'immense dog' or, as we more accurately surmise, a wolf (p. 67). Not only is he a vampire but a lycanthrope, or werewolf, as well. As becomes clear later, Dracula is a metamorph: a shape-shifter with the ability to assume the shape of many creatures. This attribute connects Dracula with many powerful figures from mythology and folk tales. This ambiguity of form plays on an underlying fear that reality and our senses are not reliable. Appearances can be deceptive. Magical disguise plays a significant part in ancient myth, religious parables, fairy tales, Gothic tales, science fiction and modern fantasy.

The description of the corpse bound to the wheel is unsettling in its gory detail and because it undermines the notion of the crucifix as protection from a vampire. The captain, as his log will substantiate, **symbolises** the notions of duty, honour and sacrifice. We also understand that the man's courage was futile. He and his crew were doomed. The journalist writes poetic prose about dead men doing their duty, but mistakes disaster for devotion. Stoker juxtaposes this supposed virtue with a rather sordid squabble over the ownership

CONTEXT

Shape-shifter legends can be found in many cultures around the world. Whether it be the Celtic selkie or the Native American Nanabozho or the Greek Zeus, the notion that the world cannot be trusted is expressed in many ways. Sometimes the shape-shifter is benign, though the monster is more often selfish and mostly malign.

CHECK THE BOOK

The Strange Case of Dr Jekyll and Mr Hyde by Robert Louis Stevenson (1886) takes the idea of shape-shifting and multiple personality and gives the Gothic novel another scientific twist.

CONTEXT

The SPCA was founded in London in 1824, the world's first official society for the protection of animals. Queen Victoria gave it the royal stamp of approval in 1840 and it rapidly expanded throughout England as the Royal Society for the Prevention of Cruelty to Animals (RSPCA).

of the ship and its cargo. He then has a little fun at the expense of dog lovers with his notion of the Whitby branch of the Society for the Prevention of Cruelty to Animals (SPCA) trying to befriend the beast.

The captain's log, introduced with a warning as to its credibility and full of *'things so strange happening'* (p. 69), is one of the few papers presented so far that employ the fragmented syntax we commonly expect of diary entries. There are incomplete sentences and entries of tantalising brevity, rapidly itemising the sequence of events on Dracula's voyage. The style develops into fuller prose as the danger looms large, and the last entry is the most sustained. The note of desperation expressed as the captain prepares to meet death 'like a man' (p. 72) recalls the end of Jonathan Harker's journal as he prepares to escape the castle (Chapter 4, p. 46).

The funeral of the sea captain unites the strands of the narrative in the location of the graveyard. Lucy is 'restless and uneasy', a dog is scared and Mr Swales is dead. Lucy's behaviour is similar to that of the dog; Stoker is deftly suggesting here that there is something animalistic in her nature which is responding to the vampire. Her sleepwalking is, in fact, a kind of awakening.

Mina thinks that Mr Swales may have 'seen Death with his dying eyes!' (p. 74). He had already seen death approaching; recalling his speech about his senses' appreciation of approaching death, the only sense he did not mention was that of touch (Chapter 6, p. 63). Stoker suggests that the look 'of fear and horror' on the old man's face was not the result of Dracula merely looking at him. Stoker underlines here the physicality of the metaphysical. Whereas Mina supposes an abstract **metaphorical** Death, perhaps in the skeletal form of the Grim Reaper, scythe in hand, we are led by Stoker to imagine Death in a more precise **personification**: Dracula.

Mina's comment about Lucy, 'I greatly fear that she is of too super-sensitive a nature to go through the world without trouble', shows her to be a good judge of character and raises an ominous note of warning (p. 74). Though Stoker voices this thought in Mina's loving and sympathetic language, it echoes the idea sown earlier that Lucy is a character whose extreme tendencies will lead her to destruction.

Mina's response to her anxiety for her friend is a prescription for healthy exercise. Stoker refrains from adding the motto '*mens sana in corpore sano*', but suggests that Lucy's mind will be made healthy if her body is healthy. This leads us to ask the question: what, then, is unhealthy about Lucy's body?

> **CONTEXT**
>
> '*Mens sana in corpore sano*', a Latin tag meaning 'a sound mind in a sound body', comes from the *Satires* of Juvenal (c.55–c.130).

CHAPTER 8

- Lucy Westenra, after sleepwalking outside at night, appears to have a small wound on her neck.
- Count Dracula's boxes are moved to Carfax.
- Mina Murray receives news of Jonathan Harker, who is safe but suffering a strange madness.
- Renfield escapes from Dr Seward's asylum but is recaptured in the grounds of Carfax.

> **GLOSSARY**
>
> 79 **apropos** to the point or purpose, with regard to something. Lucy's remark comes out of nothing and takes Mina by surprise
>
> 84 **demeanour** conduct or behaviour

Mina gives a description of Robin Hood's Bay and the walk that stimulates the appetite and exhausts both herself and Lucy Westenra. Lucy's mother invites a young curate to stay for supper, and both girls struggle to stay awake.

Three days later Mina describes discovering Lucy missing from the bedroom. Mina at first thinks it is not possible for Lucy to have left the house because she is only wearing her nightdress, but is shocked to discover the front door wide open. She follows Lucy into the night, glad it is dark and the streets empty. She races up the steps to the abbey.

She calls to Lucy, who is 'half-reclining' on the seat by the grave with a dark figure, 'long and black', leaning over her. Mina glimpses a 'white face and red, gleaming eyes' (p. 77). She reaches Lucy, who is gasping for breath and covering her throat. Mina wraps Lucy in a large shawl but later thinks she has hurt her friend's neck by accident when she spots 'two little red points like pin-pricks' on Lucy's throat (p. 78). They return home without being discovered.

Mina describes a brief interlude of happiness during the day; at night Lucy again wakes and tries to leave, but Mina has locked the door. She wakes to find Lucy, asleep, pointing at a large bat silhouetted against the moon.

Walking on the clifftop path, Lucy startles Mina by her comment 'His red eyes again!' (p. 79). For a brief moment Mina thinks she sees a dark figure in the distance, with 'great eyes like burning flames', but tells herself and Lucy it was a trick of the light. Later on she sees Lucy asleep and pale at her window with a large bird. Mrs Westenra confides in Mina that Lucy's marriage must happen soon as she, Lucy's mother, has little time left to live. Lucy herself is becoming weaker. Her neck wound is not healing, and her strange behaviour at night continues.

Solicitors' letters show that Count Dracula's boxes are being moved to Carfax.

Lucy recovers her health. She recalls the night she was sleepwalking in the graveyard and she alarms Mina by describing her soul leaving her body. Mina receives news of her fiancé at last. Jonathan Harker has been cared for in the '*Hospital of St Joseph and Ste Mary, Buda-Pesth*' for six weeks and he is no longer raving. Sister Agatha's letter has blessings and warnings for them both (pp. 83–4).

> **CONTEXT**
>
> The chemical formula for chloral hydrate ('$C_2HCl_3O.H_2O$') was discovered in 1832 and was developed as a narcotic for medical purposes from around 1870, but became a recreational drug among the middle class who could afford to indulge such pastimes.

Dr Seward describes an abrupt change in Renfield's behaviour. Haughtily he speaks of 'the Master', who is 'at hand' (p. 84). When he calms down, he makes cryptic references to the Bible. Dr Seward, still dwelling on his unrequited love for Lucy, is unable to sleep. He is taking chloral hydrate to sleep, but is aware he needs to resist his developing habitual dependence.

Renfield escapes to Carfax. As he begs to be able to serve his master, he is captured and restrained.

COMMENTARY

Some commentators see both Lucy and Mina as examples of an emerging contemporary new identity for women, embodying early feminist attitudes and challenging old ideals. But Stoker's attitude to the 'New Woman' is far from sympathetic, and it is obvious that these women are not of the same mould. Lucy has an exuberant and impulsive nature; Mina is dutiful and aware of her social obligations. This is in part due to their relative economic status. Mina is purposeful and has ambitions to write; Lucy is frivolous and has no sense of her future other than an advantageous marriage. Stoker gives each of them aspects of the 'New Woman' so scathingly mocked in the popular press at the time, but not in equal measure. Mina speaks of the 'New Woman' as if she does not see herself completely within that category: 'Some of the "New Woman" writers will some day start an idea that men and women should be allowed to see each other asleep before proposing or accepting' (p. 75).

Stoker further underlines the difference between the women by showing the relationship between them to be more like that of mother and child than friends. This is not the last time that Mina will be cast in the role of the mother figure. Mina is unaware of the danger and cannot protect Lucy from the visits of Count Dracula. Each new moment of relief is followed by a relapse into further concerns. Lucy's behaviour becomes truly alarming when she speaks of her soul leaving her body. Neither Mina nor Lucy is aware of the full portent of that description, though we sense that Mina is more worried than Lucy.

It is another note on the **theme** of religious difference that Jonathan Harker returns to full health in the care of Catholic nuns – particularly as they, being wedded to the Church, represent the exact opposite of what Lucy has just enacted: a marriage to the Antichrist.

Dr Seward, though a man of science, is not an atheist. His musings on time and God, madness and man show this clearly. He despises Renfield's madness for being a form of religious mania, in which 'he will soon think that he himself is God' (p. 85). Dr Seward sees that Renfield is not alone in the blasphemous arrogance that prevents people from truly understanding God: 'The real God taketh heed

CHECK THE NET
Talia Schaffer's article 'New Woman Novelists (1880–1910)' gives an insight into the position of women writers in the Victorian and Edwardian eras. You can read this essay online at **www.litencyc.com** – click on Topics & Events and search for the article title.

lest a sparrow fall; but the God created from human vanity sees no difference between an eagle and a sparrow.' This may seem an unusual attitude for a scientist, in the century when Charles Darwin's *On the Origin of Species by Means of Natural Selection* (1859) polarised the realms of religion and of science, but the controversy also resulted in many scientists adopting an agnostic view. Dr Seward represents the wavering allegiance of the agnostic, sceptical and unwilling to believe. He is scientific in his approach, but when later confronted with things he cannot explain, he will accept that faith is an important part of his philosophy. Stoker is carefully preparing the ground here for further developments in this character. He is an essentially good person who is suffering a loss of faith or a crisis in his belief.

Renfield's remark on bridesmaids losing their appeal when the bride appears seems to unite both the religious and sexual themes of this chapter in its quasi-biblical riddling language. It implies that soon Renfield will not have to settle for second best, which is the unfortunate position Dr Seward, as a rejected suitor, feels most keenly. The terminology of marriage is swiftly translated into thoughts of Lucy that keep him awake.

Stoker subtly suggests that Dr Seward is at risk of becoming addicted to chloral hydrate, a fashionable narcotic of the time, easily available to the medical profession. It is another example of Dr Seward being a modern man of science, as the drug was particularly developed for use in the treatment of insanity. Dr Seward's private asylum was typical of the care afforded to patients with symptoms of mental ill health.

Renfield's restrained excitement is less obviously sexual in nature, though perhaps becomes more extreme in the hints that Stoker gives us at the end of the chapter. Renfield's shrieks of 'It is coming – coming – coming!' form a double entendre that heightens our sense of him as a man at the edge of normal human behaviour (p. 86). His willingness to be enslaved and the fact that he is bound in a 'strait-waistcoat' are suggestive of sadomasochistic fetishism.

The parallel Stoker creates between the eccentric behaviour of Lucy and the outright insanity of Renfield is striking. Both escape from

CHECK THE NET

For a comprehensive history of medical and social attitudes, including literary detail, see the Mental Health History Timeline maintained by Andrew Roberts at the Middlesex University website. Go to **www.mdx.ac.uk/www/study** and click on the Mental Health and Learning Disability link. The entries on the timeline for the 1890s are especially relevant to *Dracula*.

their caring guardians at night and roam at large in their nightgowns; both are drawn to Dracula. It is yet another **ironic** coincidence that Dr Seward will be the one to care for them both, without understanding either.

See **Text 2** of **Extended commentaries** for further discussion of part of this chapter.

CHAPTER 9

- Mina Murray and Jonathan Harker are married; they agree never to discuss Jonathan's adventures abroad.
- Renfield escapes again to the grounds of Carfax.
- Dr Abraham Van Helsing is consulted about Lucy Westenra's mysterious illness.
- Lucy takes a sudden turn for the worse.

GLOSSARY

93 **boudoir** a genteel eighteenth-century term for a room where a lady may be alone or entertain her intimate friends, derived from the French expression for 'a place to sulk in'

94 **arbitrary** opinionated or inclined to argument, especially in the sense of dismissing other views

Mina Harker describes her husband's condition in a letter to her friend Lucy Westenra. Jonathan Harker has been raving but the nuns will not reveal what he has said. Jonathan gives Mina his notebook; he does not wish to remember what it contains, but invites her to read it. Mina wants to know what happened to him but does not read the journal. She wishes to show Jonathan that she trusts him, so the book is sealed shut as her wedding present to him. Mina writes of duty and happiness, suggesting Lucy must follow her example to know true happiness in marriage.

Lucy replies describing her healthy activities and happiness with Arthur Holmwood in Whitby. She is no longer sleepwalking. She writes briefly about her love for Arthur and their forthcoming wedding.

Dr Seward records his observations of Renfield, who is no longer interested in being given a kitten. The patient has violent fits for three days, though he is calm at night. He is allowed to escape as an experiment but does not take the opportunity, escaping instead at a moment of his choice. Renfield is caught again by the door to Carfax chapel. The attendants restrain Renfield and stop him attacking Dr Seward. A large bat is seen flying away, 'straight on, as if it knew where it was bound for or had some intention of its own' (p. 91). Renfield becomes ominously calm.

CONTEXT

The psychological approach to the Gothic **genre** examines the relationship between conscious and unconscious apprehension of reality. The dream, in its Gothic context, is a realm where the ego, the consciousness of the self, is broken down and the restraints of civilised behaviour are removed. The inarticulate and incoherent imagination of unacknowledged urges adds to the sense of chaos and 'losing one's grip'. The notion that there is significance in dreams that can be interpreted has a long history.

Lucy begins a diary in conscious imitation of her friend Mina. She is now at Hillingham and she writes of the return of her troubling dreams. She is not sleeping well. An exchange of letters and telegrams follows between Arthur Holmwood and Dr Seward. Arthur invites Dr Seward to examine Lucy, before being called away to his family home because his father is unwell. Dr Seward is baffled by Lucy's condition and takes the opportunity, when she cuts herself on some broken glass, of obtaining some of her blood to test. The test shows her blood to be normal and healthy. Dr Seward explains to Arthur his intention to call in Dr Abraham Van Helsing. Van Helsing agrees to come at once, in response to the request from his old friend and student. He is guarded in his view of Lucy's illness, and returns home to think over the cause of her disease. In the meantime Dr Seward agrees to keep a close watch over Lucy.

Renfield is restless and violent again. He complains of being deserted and resumes his diet of flies. He has screaming fits at noon and sunset, but by night is no longer interested in keeping flies.

Three telegrams from Dr Seward to Van Helsing record Lucy's initial recovery and then a terrible change for the worse. Van Helsing is summoned urgently to help.

COMMENTARY

This chapter continues to increase the threat from the unseen Dracula. A sense of alien menace dominates the narrative without any explicit reference to horrific or terrible events. The reader is consistently placed in a position of sustained **ironic** observation by the fragmented narrative and shifting perspectives. This chapter is the point at which Dr Seward begins to take over the burden of responsibility for the narrative. A sequence of coincidences advances the plot.

Jonathan Harker's experiences, the first four chapters of the novel and the whole of Dracula's evil plan, are sealed away in a notebook to be forgotten. Jonathan's 'brain fever' (p. 88), a form of amnesia, helps prevent connections being made at this stage between characters suffering similar experiences. Mina is no longer around to protect Lucy, who moves into greater danger near London. We are alert now to the ways in which Dracula's influence over Lucy and Renfield is shown, and we understand the significance of the unusually large bat seen by Dr Seward. In this chapter Stoker introduces the character who represents the hope of resisting Dracula and who will go on to be the architect of their salvation.

Van Helsing is only briefly introduced by Dr Seward, who calls him in, first of all, as an expert in rare diseases. Van Helsing is 'seemingly arbitrary', a 'philosopher and a metaphysician, and one of the most advanced scientists of his day' (p. 94). Dr Seward has total confidence in his old master. Van Helsing has an open mind, strong nerves and a cool temper. He is resolute, self-possessed and tolerant; he is also kind, true-hearted and sympathetic.

Stoker has created here the moral opposite of Count Dracula. But Van Helsing and Dracula have many qualities in common. Both are powerful and strong-willed; both are determined and resourceful. Both are dedicated to strange wisdom and esoteric philosophy. They both speak in forms of English that immediately characterise them as foreigners. The absolute distinction between them is apparent in the immediate and obvious impressions given of each character. Dracula is a fearsome, cruel and unsympathetic aristocrat; Van Helsing is a healer doing 'noble work … for mankind' (p. 94).

The marriage of Jonathan Harker and Mina Murray is a typical example of how Mina embodies the notions of duty, faith and endurance. Despite her own desire to understand Jonathan's madness, she rejects the opportunity to gain knowledge and turns her ignorance into a **symbolic** bond of trust between them. It is not, in her view, for the wife to question her husband about his past.

> **CONTEXT**
>
> A metaphysician is a student or specialist in philosophy, with particular interest in the theory of knowledge and abstract concepts (sometimes interpreted as an interest in occult mysteries).

Her reasoning for this subservience is a concern for his mental well-being. The notebook is sealed under the impression of the wedding ring, given to Harker as his wedding gift and blessed with a kiss. The contrast between this chaste kiss representing the sacred union of their marriage and the more eroticised kiss of the women described in the notebook emphasises the virtue of Mina. She is happy to be suffering the pain of not knowing the truth as a sacrifice for her love.

It is possible to see Mina's act of self-denial here as an example of female virtue in contrast to the **archetypical** view of woman as the instrument of man's fall from grace. Unlike the mythical Eve in the Garden of Eden who is tempted into the forbidden pursuit of knowledge, Mina remains in a state of blissful ignorance. It could be a suggestion that Mina is worthy of a place in paradise and it does reinforce the contrast between the two main female characters. Mina is a virtual saint in martyrdom in comparison with Lucy, who describes her pastimes, and her feelings for Arthur, in a much more frivolous tone.

Mina is still aware of herself as a model for Lucy and of Lucy's need for guidance: 'I want you to see now … whither duty has led me' (p. 89). Lucy's reference to her 'appetite like a cormorant' is another example of the erratic nature of this character: the cormorant is supposed to have an insatiable appetite. Her remark shows the continuing impact of Dracula's influence upon her and her susceptibility to his corruption. It appears in her short note celebrating her recovery and is just enough to give the happy picture she creates an unsettling note of physical self-indulgence: 'Arthur says I am getting fat' (p. 89). Lucy's diary shows her trying to imitate her friend, but she lacks the real urge to be a writer that drives Mina. She seems mostly concerned that Arthur will be upset by the change in her appearance.

Arthur Holmwood's invitation to Dr Seward suggests that he fears some form of insanity and is concerned to be discreet. He is calling in a specialist in madness, a friend and defeated rival for his fiancée's affections. The fragile health of Lucy's mother and Arthur's father places both Lucy and Arthur in the ascendancy as representatives of the next generation of their class; they are about to come into their

CHECK THE BOOK

See *The Madwoman in the Attic: The Woman Writer and the Nineteenth-Century Literary Imagination* by Sandra M. Gilbert and Susan Gubar (1979) for a discussion of the influence of masculine attitudes on the perceptions of women writers. The feminist perspective can be useful when considering, for example, Stoker's depiction of the female characters and the identification of insanity as an unmanly thing in *Dracula*.

own as inheritors of wealth and social status. The coincidences of ill health and discretion also play their part in furthering the plot development. Mrs Westenra's ignorance and weak heart will be important factors in later events, and the imminent death of Arthur's father takes Arthur out of events at Hillingham. Lucy is left protected only by the overtired and morose Dr Seward.

The description given by Dr Seward of London in the sunset is dominated by his 'desolate heart' (p. 97). He is fascinated by the appearance of 'smoky beauty' in the foul atmosphere and his own isolation in the 'breathing misery' of the insane asylum. Stoker manages to capture Dr Seward's melancholy and convey a sense of the modern metropolis as the centre of civilisation that Dracula threatens.

CHAPTER 10

- Arthur Holmwood gives his blood to Lucy Westenra by transfusion.
- Dr Seward leaves Lucy unprotected at night.
- Now it is Dr Seward's turn to give his blood to Lucy.
- Van Helsing decorates Lucy's bedroom with garlic.

Dr Seward allays Mrs Westenra's fears about Van Helsing. Van Helsing advises Dr Seward not to share his opinions about Lucy's illness with Arthur Holmwood; they must wait and see what happens. Van Helsing advises him to keep his casebook in detail: 'We learn from failure, not from success!' (p. 100). Lucy's mother is worried but remains calm; Dr Seward notices that she seems to have taken the news of Lucy's illness without too much anxiety. He speaks of his knowledge of 'spiritual pathology' that leads him to insist she does not spend time with Lucy.

Lucy is seen by Van Helsing, who is shocked by her condition and prescribes an immediate blood transfusion as a matter of life or death. Dr Seward volunteers, but then Arthur Holmwood arrives and at Van Helsing's request gives his blood to Lucy. Following the

CHECK THE BOOK

The plot of Charlotte Brontë's *Jane Eyre*, published in 1847, depends upon the concealment and revelation of madness. The nineteenth-century fear of mental disorder is famously linked in this novel to the idea of the female as the hysterical woman, to be controlled, cured or contained.

GLOSSARY

103 **trituration** a medical term for the vigorous mixing of liquids or solids to produce a single substance, rather like stirring a cup of tea to help the sugar dissolve

109 **pharmacopoeia** an official list of medicines and drugs, with their uses and dosages.

CONTEXT

One of the earliest accounts of the circulation of blood was by an Arabic physician Ibn Al-Nafis in 1260. This was more than two hundred and fifty years before William Harvey's treatise on the circulation of blood around the body, which was published in 1628. The first human blood transfusion was performed in Paris by the Frenchman Jean-Baptiste Denis in June 1667. A number of fatal reactions led to the banning of all transfusions in France and England. The first successful human blood transfusion took place in 1818.

transfusion, Van Helsing notices the wound on Lucy's neck but sends Arthur home before letting Dr Seward examine it. That same night Van Helsing returns to Amsterdam to consult his books, warning Dr Seward to be vigilant in his care of Lucy while he is away: 'If you leave her, and harm befall, you shall not sleep easy hereafter!' (p. 104).

Lucy is afraid to sleep because of the horrors of her dreams, and Dr Seward promises to wake her at the first sign of disturbance. Relieved, Lucy sleeps easily. The next day, Dr Seward returns to work, tired. The following night, Lucy stops him from keeping his vigil, and instead he sleeps. He is woken the next morning by Van Helsing, and they discover to their horror that Lucy has suffered another relapse and is 'more horribly white and wan-looking than ever' (p. 106). A second blood transfusion is needed, and Dr Seward is proud to give his blood to save Lucy.

Van Helsing orders 'white flowers' for Lucy (p. 108) and explains the medicinal purpose of the garlic. He decorates the room with the garlic flowers, much to Dr Seward's surprise, who considers Van Helsing's actions 'odd, and not to be found in any pharmacopoeia' (p. 109) and asks if he is working 'some spell to keep out an evil spirit' (p. 110). Van Helsing insists on all doors and windows being closed, and then he and Dr Seward leave Lucy to rest.

COMMENTARY

In this chapter Dr Seward becomes the main **narrator** and retains this position for much of the rest of the novel. He assumes a directing role in the Westenra household and is clearly conscious of the psychological aspects of Mrs Westenra's condition. The reference to 'spiritual pathology' (p. 100) indicates the state of development of psychology and is not necessarily a willingness on his part to consider some mystical or religious cause for her condition or Lucy's.

Van Helsing clearly knows more than his pupil, but does not share his thoughts entirely with Dr Seward. In his reticence he can be seen to follow the advice he gives others. He is cautious and wise in making and sharing his understanding of the situation. Van Helsing's return to Amsterdam later in the chapter connects him with the world of learning and esoteric knowledge, but it is not the learning of an English gentleman. There is a suggestion of mysterious knowledge in Van Helsing's background. To a degree, this places him in the role of the sage or the wise man. His actions at the end of the chapter make him seem much more the mystic than the scientist.

The blood transfusions to save Lucy's life will also form a direct connection between all the major characters. It seems obvious to state that blood, with all its **metaphorical** connotations, is at the heart of this novel. Arthur Holmwood, fittingly the first donor, as Lucy's fiancé, has aristocratic 'blood so pure' and is 'so young and strong' that they do not need to 'defibrinate' his blood (p. 102). Unlike Dracula, the despotic foreign aristocrat, Arthur is a noble English gentleman. Dr Seward as a mere scientist belongs to the class that 'toil much in the world of thought', but is still young and strong (p. 102).

Van Helsing insists Dr Seward must give precedence to Arthur, but allows him to be the next to give his blood for Lucy. Again the question of discretion is raised as Van Helsing fears Arthur may be frightened and jealous on discovering another man has given blood to his fiancée. There is an underlying intimacy to the act of sharing bodily fluids that cannot be avoided, and Van Helsing is the first to bring it into the open. Dr Seward's eagerness to contribute ('No man knows till he experiences it, what it is to feel his own life-blood drawn away into the veins of the woman he loves') and rather pathetic envy of Arthur's greater contribution ('You took a great deal more from Art') are further hints of their awareness of inappropriate intimacy (p. 107). Stoker makes no mention of the possibly fatal consequences of mismatching blood groups.

It is Dr Seward who assumes the responsibilities of protecting Lucy. The **irony** here operates at many levels. The most significant is that Lucy prevents Dr Seward from watching over her at night.

CONTEXT

In Arthurian legends it is Merlin who fulfils the role of wise man, and, in J. R. R. Tolkien's *The Lord of the Rings* (1954–5), Gandalf.

CONTEXT

Fibrin, a protein compound found in blood, has to be removed to enable blood to flow without clots. In 1873 Sir Thomas Smith of St Bartholomew's Hospital, London, successfully transfused defibrinated blood. In 1901 Karl Landsteiner described three different human blood types: A, B and O; and Alfred von Decastello and Adriano Sturli defined a fourth type, AB, in 1902. Landsteiner argued that his work could be helpful in improving blood transfusion practice, but his ideas were ignored for over a decade.

Her happy thoughts of Arthur follow her description of a physical presence 'warm about me' (p. 106). She says she is thinking of Arthur, but there is a hint of sexual energy to these thoughts that is closer to the surface than before. We anticipate the next development that follows Lucy's obvious vulnerability and are not surprised by her relapse.

CHAPTER 11

- Mrs Westenra removes the garlic from Lucy's room.
- Van Helsing gives his blood to Lucy by transfusion.
- An escaped wolf breaks into Lucy's bedroom.
- Mrs Westenra dies of shock, leaving Lucy alone to meet her terrible fate.

GLOSSARY

117 **quondam** Latin for 'formerly' or 'at one time'. Its use here emphasises the journalist's educated perspective and expectations of his readership in contrast with the language of the zookeeper and his wife

Lucy feels comforted by the attention of Van Helsing and is ready to sleep now, without fear; in the garlic's smell she finds 'peace' (p. 111).

The following day Van Helsing and Dr Seward return to find that her mother has interfered with arrangements, opening a window and removing the garlic. Van Helsing talks of being frustrated by fate and of being ready to fight the devil; he is not surprised to find Lucy is again unwell. A third blood transfusion is necessary, and this time Van Helsing gives Lucy his blood. Afterwards he warns Mrs Westenra not to interfere with his 'system of cure' (p. 112). Dr Seward is perturbed by events, and questions his own sanity.

Lucy describes Van Helsing's vigil at her bedside as 'Four days and nights of peace'; and as a result she is recovering again. As he sleeps, she is aware of bats 'or something' flapping angrily at the window (p. 113). But Van Helsing then has to depart again for Amsterdam.

The narrative leaps ahead to the next day. A journalist reports his interview with a zookeeper about an escaped wolf. The zookeeper is at first reluctant to talk to the journalist, but a bribe loosens his tongue, and he describes the wolf and talks of a tall stranger with 'a 'ard, cold look and red eyes' who seems to terrify the normally fierce wolf (p. 115). As the interview concludes, the surprisingly tame wolf appears at the window, its head full of broken glass.

The narrative then leaps back to the previous night, when Renfield attacks Dr Seward, cuts him and drinks his blood. He repeatedly shouts, 'The blood is the life!' (p. 118). Dr Seward, 'over-excited and weary', rests at his asylum. Van Helsing's telegram advising Dr Seward to watch over Lucy that night is misdirected and arrives late. Dr Seward rushes to her the next day full of dismay; he fears there is 'some horrible doom hanging over us', and is all too aware of what he will find.

Lucy faces death, but manages to record the events of the night, in her diary, motivated by an impulse to take responsibility for what has happened. She hears a flapping at the window and a distant howl. Her mother, uneasy about her daughter, joins her in the bedroom. Suddenly a wolf breaks through the window, and Lucy's mother dies of shock. As she dies, she clutches at the garlic wreath around her daughter's neck, tearing it away. Lucy sees some moving specks of dust swirling in the darkness, and loses consciousness. When she stirs again, she calls her maids, who rush in. Knowing they are all afraid, she instructs them to go and drink some wine. She later discovers them all unconscious, as the wine has been drugged with her mother's medicine.

Lucy is now alone, and the 'floating' specks return (p. 120). She writes her farewell note and hides it, not expecting to survive.

COMMENTARY

The chapter opens with Lucy Westenra writing in her diary about the wonderful Van Helsing and how she is almost scared of his 'fierce' (p. 110) manner. Although she enjoys better sleep, the comparison to Ophelia, suggested by the flowers strewn around her, is not a happy thought. Ophelia is a melancholy figure who, obedient to her father's wishes, breaks off her relationship with

---

CONTEXT

It is **ironic** that Lucy should choose to quote from *Hamlet* (V.1.230–1) here. Ophelia at this point in Shakespeare's play is dead, her corpse about to be buried. Gertrude scatters flowers over her coffin, saying: 'I thought thy bride-bed to have deck'd, sweet maid, / And not have strew'd thy grave' (V.1.243–4).

CONTEXT

There are many references and allusions to Shakespeare plays in *Dracula*, particularly *Hamlet*. As well as this reference in Chapter 11, there are direct quotes from the play in Chapter 3 (p. 32, taken from I.5.107) and Chapter 20 (p. 225: 'to "be cruel only to be kind"', III.4.180), and a further allusion in Chapter 6 (p. 59: 'There is a method in his madness' from 'Though this be madness, yet there is method in't', II.2.205–6).

Hamlet and then later drowns herself. It suggests a certain histrionic sensibility on Lucy's part in identifying with this character, or perhaps a lack of self-knowledge, as it is unlikely she would so readily play the dutiful daughter. The macabre note is, however, entirely apt for the opening of this chapter in which she unwittingly plays out the last part of her mortal existence.

Mrs Westenra, becoming unusually anxious about Lucy in the night, goes against the instructions of Van Helsing and removes the garlic flowers, being afraid of their adverse effect on Lucy in her 'weak state', and opens a window (p. 111). She thus becomes the device by which Dracula succeeds in thwarting Van Helsing and gaining access to Lucy once more. Is Mrs Westenra acting under the hypnotic influence of Dracula? This is possible, though Stoker makes no suggestion that she has acted out of character. Equally, it is at least plausible that her actions are those of a doting mother. But if we recall the previous chapter where Dr Seward describes Mrs Westenra's apparent detachment from the reality of Lucy's illness, her behaviour seems slightly suspect. This also avoids the other reasonable suspicion that Stoker's tale is becoming over-reliant on a sequence of extraordinary coincidences.

Van Helsing understands the significance of her actions immediately and seems to suffer a moment of personal crisis. Dr Seward records, with appropriate alarm, the sight of his mentor having a 'break down' and being overcome with 'mute despair' (p. 111). Van Helsing is now directly involved in the struggle, which he describes in significantly ominous fashion: 'How are all the powers of the devils against us!' (p. 112). He peremptorily dismisses Dr Seward's offer to provide blood for Lucy and gives his own as a sacrifice to the conflict with the devil. He then takes on the responsibility of watching over Lucy himself. Where the young men have, in each case, been sent home to sleep off the effects of the transfusion, Van Helsing intends to stay up over the next two nights, watching over his patient.

The rapid leaps in the chronological sequence gain coherence when Dracula appears at the zoo. His purpose becomes clear at the moment the wolf smashes through Lucy's window. Initially, the interview with the zookeeper seems an odd change of pace and location, with little connection to the foregoing focus on Lucy. The evident comedy of the scene is at odds with the gathering pace of the attack on Lucy.

Stoker allows the journalist to use a particular form of phonetic representation for the zookeeper's accent during the interview, presenting a very clearly class-conscious view of the keeper. This cockney-speaking ruffian and his wife belong in the tradition of exaggerated, humorous caricatures of working-class types. The zookeeper may be uneducated but he is sharp enough to make a bit of money out of the journalist.

Despite the digressive quality of this slight interlude of comic relief, which pits the wits of the middle-class journalist against the self-serving inclinations of the zookeeper, the interview reveals to us the fact that Dracula has been to visit the wolves in the zoo. The zookeeper is allowed a little comment on the stranger being 'as perlite as a lord' (p. 115), which reminds us that Dracula has achieved one of his aims expressed to Harker in the early chapters: he wanted to avoid losing his status as a 'master', a recognised member of the upper or ruling class. There is a rather telling remark from the zookeeper: 'I did not like the airs as he give 'isself' (p. 115). This shows a form of class-conscious aversion to the Count's haughty manner but also suggests that the encounter unsettled him in other ways.

Dr Seward's injury by Renfield takes him out of the way. It is clear that this is now part of an orchestrated plan by Dracula to remove all the protective barriers between himself and Lucy. Renfield's sudden violence and bloodlust is a prelude to the bloodletting that will take Lucy's life. His shrieks of 'The blood is the life!' are a perverted reminder of the ritual of Holy Communion (p. 118). It is also a moment of revelation that Dr Seward is too shocked to connect with his previous observations of Renfield's eating habits. Renfield may have consumed the flies and birds whole, but he was really interested in their blood. This is, however, the only blood spilt that is described in the chapter.

By the time we read Lucy's note, we know her fate has been sealed. We read on, anticipating the climax of the vampire's embrace.

CHECK THE BOOK
The Working Classes in Victorian Fiction by P. J. Keating (1971) gives a helpful overview of the ways Victorian writers use language to define class perspectives in their work.

CONTEXT
In the service of Communion, Christian worshippers take a consecrated wafer and some wine which **symbolically** represent the body and blood of Christ. By consuming these, Christians reaffirm their faith and participate in the life of the Church.

The first few lines seem to indicate an altruistic impulse that seems at odds with her previous character. Caring about unspecified 'others' instead of herself has not really been part of her outlook so far. It may be an indication of a guilty conscience or some form of intuition that she will go on to become a threat to those who love her. Her description of 'a whole myriad of little specks' which blow through the broken window and circle round the room 'like the pillar of dust that travellers describe when there is a simoom in the desert' (p. 119) recalls Harker's experiences at Castle Dracula. With the maids drugged and her mother dead, she finds herself alone, with just a few moments to write her note, prevented from leaving the house by the wolf and surrounded by those 'specks' (p. 120).

Stoker leaves out the anticipated 'kiss' at this point. It might be that Stoker is withholding the full horror of the spectacle of Dracula at work for the later assault on Mina. In this way, the whole build-up to Lucy's death is an elaborate teasing of the reader. We really want to see what Dracula can do, but he remains an insubstantial figure haunting the narrative. The man with no reflection is glimpsed only through the reports of those who do not yet know him. We have not yet seen him being a vampire, sucking the blood of his victim. Why has Lucy not recalled any of the visits from Dracula as clearly as Harker recalls the half-waking, half-dreaming passionate embrace with his vampire? It does draw attention to the fact that, so far, only one clear and full account of the vampire's kiss from the viewpoint of the victim has appeared in this collection of papers, and it is from a male perspective.

CONTEXT

A word of Arabic origin (from *samūm* meaning 'poisonous'), a simoom is a hot, dry, seasonal wind that blows sand across the deserts of Arabia and North Africa, making it hard for travellers to breathe.

CHAPTER 12

- Quincey Morris gives his blood to Lucy Westenra by transfusion.
- Lucy's teeth appear to be sharper than before.
- Arthur Holmwood, following the death of his father, becomes Lord Godalming.
- Lucy dies.

Dr Seward arrives first at Hillingham, but cannot find a way into the house. Van Helsing arrives and together they break in; there they find the bodies of the drugged maids. They discover Mrs Westenra, dead; there is still faint hope for Lucy, and Van Helsing fights desperately to save her.

As they work to save Lucy's life, a gentleman arrives from Arthur Holmwood but his admittance is postponed. Van Helsing battles in 'deadly earnest'; he speaks as though he is playing a game of chess with the devil: 'The first gain is ours! Check to the king!' (p. 123). Van Helsing takes care to hide her wound and Lucy is left in the care of a maid as he and Dr Seward discuss what to do. They decide more blood is needed but, exhausted, they cannot give more themselves nor can they ask the servants to provide. Quincey Morris, the man who has been sent by Arthur Holmwood, volunteers to give his blood to Lucy in the fourth transfusion, despite being in the dark about her condition.

Van Helsing discovers the note written by Lucy; Dr Seward on reading it wonders if Lucy is mad, but Van Helsing dismisses this idea. As he looks after Lucy, Quincey Morris questions Dr Seward about her loss of blood, wondering where 'the blood of four strong men' has gone over the last ten days (p. 126). Dr Seward is unable to answer him: 'That … is the crux … I can't even hazard a guess' (p. 126). Quincey speaks about how he has seen vampire bats sucking the blood of cattle in Argentina.

As dusk approaches, Lucy mimes tearing paper in her sleep under the thoughtful gaze of Van Helsing. Asleep she seems stronger, and her teeth are changing, becoming sharper. Arthur's arrival revives Lucy slightly, but Dr Seward observes that she will not recover this time.

Stoker now introduces a switch in scene. Jonathan and Mina Harker have returned to Exeter and are living happily together. Mina wishes this happiness for Lucy in a letter that her friend will never read.

GLOSSARY

133 **ejaculation** the word has changed its meaning somewhat since the end of the nineteenth century, and is used here to suggest a sudden involuntary expression of shock

134 **pathos** a melancholy expression of sadness that arouses a sympathetic response in the spectator

CONTEXT

The word 'crux' has two meanings: the more usual and intended meaning here is a puzzle or something that is difficult to explain; the other is from the Latin word for cross – a possible religious significance?

A doctor reports to Dr Seward on Renfield's condition, and reveals that Dracula's boxes are being moved from Carfax. Renfield escapes, and before he can be recaptured in a violent struggle, he hurts the workers moving the boxes; they are only placated when the doctor gives them some strong drink and some money.

Mina writes, again in vain, to Lucy to explain that, after the death of Jonathan's employer, they are now very wealthy. Arthur's father also dies, and he becomes Lord Godalming.

> **CONTEXT**
> Lucy's breathing is described more than once in this chapter as being 'stertorous', emphasising the noisy and laboured sound she makes while she is sleeping.

Dr Seward relieves Van Helsing in his watch over Lucy and notices a large bat. Lucy is different when sleeping and awake; Dr Seward comments upon her 'odd' and 'curious' attitude to the garlic: 'whenever she got into that lethargic state, with the stertorous breathing, she put the flowers from her; but ... when she waked she clutched them close' (p. 133). When Van Helsing returns, he notices that her neck wound has vanished, and he predicts her death. He prepares Lucy for a last visit from Arthur, who keeps a vigil at her bedside as she drifts back off to sleep.

Dr Seward notices the 'strange change' (p. 134) come over Lucy again, and suddenly she calls for Arthur to kiss her. But Arthur is prevented from responding by Van Helsing, who drags him back 'with a fury of strength' that startles Seward. A 'spasm as of rage' crosses Lucy's face before she drifts off again. When she wakes, she seems to plead with Van Helsing, calling him 'My true friend' and asking him 'with untellable pathos' to 'guard him, and give him peace!' (p. 134). Now Arthur is allowed to kiss her forehead.

Lucy dies, and Arthur is led away, overcome by grief. Van Helsing and Dr Seward are left alone with Lucy, who seems to have undergone another remarkable change. Lucy, though dead, seems in her appearance to be full of life. Van Helsing declares that this is 'only the beginning' but refuses to explain himself to Dr Seward, who again must 'Wait and see' (p. 135).

COMMENTARY

In this chapter, three deaths lead to inheritances that benefit the main characters, but these are incidental to the main action of the chapter, which is the slow build-up to the moment of Lucy's death.

The discovery of Lucy and her mother's corpse is described by Dr Seward. Again the competence of the young doctor is overshadowed by the resourcefulness of his mentor; Dr Seward is unable to gain access to the house without Van Helsing's advice and equipment. Their attempts to save Lucy's life are conducted in an atmosphere of disorder and chaos. The servants of the house are roused to assist and sternly brought back from the edge of panic and hysteria. Dr Seward is shown to be capable of dealing firmly with the servants as necessary and appropriate to the situation, urging them into action still 'half-clad' (p. 122). But these characters are incidental and, having drawn the blinds to observe the 'etiquette of death' (p. 123), they are forgotten.

Again Stoker relies on coincidence to draw another character back into the narrative at this point. He gives Quincey Morris a false entrance under the cover of the confusion of the household. It is the most immense good fortune for the doctors, being in need of fresh blood, that the representative of the New World happens to be around to volunteer. The business is barely brought up in conversation before Quincey is offering to open his veins for Lucy. He also recovers swiftly, with a glass of wine, communicating the situation to Arthur by telegram and quizzing Dr Seward on the truth of the matter. Quincey is the first to articulate the sensible and obvious question about the quantity of blood that has passed through Lucy's veins in recent days: 'What took it out?' (p. 126).

The order in which the men have given their lifeblood for Lucy's sake is not a matter of circumstance. First, the pure blood of the English aristocrat, Arthur Holmwood; second, the blood of the English educated professional middle class, Dr Seward; third, the old blood of European philosopher Van Helsing; and last, the young blood of the Wild West. This is an arrangement of old alliances against the new threat to Western civilisation arising in the East. It also indicates a notion of who might be worthy of

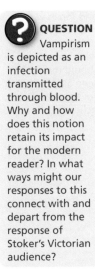

QUESTION
Vampirism is depicted as an infection transmitted through blood. Why and how does this notion retain its impact for the modern reader? In what ways might our responses to this connect with and depart from the response of Stoker's Victorian audience?

mingling their blood with the blood of an Englishwoman of noble or, at least, genteel birth.

Mina's two unread letters to Lucy do one very important thing for the furtherance of the plot: they establish the financial independence of Jonathan and Mina Harker and in so doing raise them up to a status of social equality with the other characters. This also provides them with the means to pursue their activities against their enemy later on. A similar independence of means is bestowed on Arthur by the death of his father.

It is another astonishing moment of narrative convenience that the madman, Renfield, manages to escape yet again from his captivity into the grounds of Carfax. Renfield is motivated to attack the workers moving Dracula's boxes because he fears they are taking away his opportunity for immortality: 'I'll fight for my Lord and Master!' (p. 130). He understands the significance of the boxes being moved out of Carfax. But it is necessary for Stoker to create a trail in order that the boxes can be traced later in the novel, and so the doctor reporting the case provides names and addresses for those involved. He also confirms the form, established in the interview with the zookeeper in the previous chapter, that the 'lower classes' find work a very thirst-provoking business and are always on the scrounge for beer money or a stiff drink. This gag will be repeated on almost every occasion the men encounter their social inferiors.

? QUESTION
Dracula persuades, coerces and forces various characters to serve his purposes. To what extent should they be seen as responsible for their own actions?

Dr Seward notices how Lucy's canine teeth seem to be 'longer and sharper' than before but puts this down to 'some trick of the light' (p. 132). Van Helsing is careful to prevent Arthur getting too close to Lucy, as he evidently anticipates the transformation that takes place just before she dies. Her instruction to Arthur – 'Kiss me!' – is clearly signalled to the reader as the desire of a vampire by the use of that one word, 'voluptuous', that Stoker reserves exclusively for the most heightened moments of vampire activity (p. 134). Arthur is saved by the violent and speedy reactions of Van Helsing: 'Not for your life! ... not for your living soul and hers!' They witness a spasm of rage in Lucy's face in response to that frustrated desire. Arthur is only allowed one chaste kiss of blessing on her forehead.

Lucy's request to Van Helsing – 'give him peace!' – could be simply a reference to Arthur (p. 134). She desires her fiancé to be relieved of his suffering. Perhaps she is asking Van Helsing to release her from the curse of vampirism; indeed, Van Helsing suggests this later on. But beyond this understanding, it is also possible she may be making a plea on behalf of Dracula, signifying the complete transfer of her allegiance. Whether Lucy is asking for Dracula to be given the peace of eternal rest or asking Van Helsing to make some form of truce with the vampire is part of the ambiguity that Stoker allows in her last words.

CHAPTER 13

- Dr Seward and Arthur Holmwood notice how, in death, Lucy Westenra still appears beautiful and full of life.
- Jonathan Harker sees a young Count Dracula in London.
- Van Helsing has a hysterical fit of laughter after Lucy's funeral.
- Children in Hampstead are found to have strange neck wounds.

> **GLOSSARY**
>
> **135 obsequious** the word has lost something of its original meaning, to be respectful of the dead, and now suggests a fawning or cringing servility
>
> **137 premonitory** warning
>
> **139 intestacy** when someone dies without making a will, the question of inheritance is open to dispute

Preparations are made for Lucy's funeral by Dr Seward; Arthur is attending his father's funeral. The undertaker's assistant comments, 'She makes a very beautiful corpse' (p. 135). Van Helsing takes charge of Lucy's writing to prevent it falling into the hands of strangers. Having taken care of the legal processes, Van Helsing and Dr Seward are able to rest.

Before retiring for the night they look again at Lucy. Dr Seward finds it difficult to believe he is looking at a corpse. Van Helsing puts wild garlic flowers on the bed and a golden crucifix on Lucy's mouth. He explains that he wants to cut off her head and remove her heart. Dr Seward, startled, asks why. Van Helsing recalls the way she changed and the promise he made to her just before her death, and he asks Dr Seward to trust him. Noticing one of Lucy's maids enter her room just before he goes to bed, Dr Seward is touched by her apparent devotion to her dead mistress. In the morning, however,

Van Helsing reveals that the maid has stolen the golden crucifix, forcing him to postpone his plans to deal with Lucy.

CHECK THE FILM
Quentin Tarantino's screenplay for *From Dusk Till Dawn* (1996) sees George Clooney and Harvey Keitel stumbling across a bar full of vampires in a violently explosive mixture of cinematic **genres**.

All the Westenra family's wealth is left to Arthur. When Arthur arrives, he grieves for Lucy with Dr Seward, and they notice how beautiful she appears in death. Arthur is 'shaken with doubt' and asks, 'Jack, is she really dead?' (p. 140). While they dine, Arthur affirms his friendship with and his trust in Van Helsing, for Lucy's sake; he gives Van Helsing permission to read Lucy's papers. That night, Van Helsing watches over Lucy's coffin, which is decorated with garlic, lilies and roses.

Mina and Jonathan Harker also attend a funeral. Hawkins, their benefactor, is buried in London; and while they are there, Jonathan spots Dracula in the street. Dracula 'has grown young', and this makes Harker both anxious and confused (p. 143), but after a brief sleep he seems to forget the incident. Mina is concerned and reconsiders reading his journal. She is informed of Lucy's death in a telegram sent by Van Helsing.

Dr Seward takes up the narrative again and recounts Lucy's funeral, where Van Helsing has a fit of hysterical giggling. Dr Seward is offended when Van Helsing compares the blood transfusions to marriage, thus suggesting Lucy has 'married' four men. Lucy is buried in Hampstead cemetery.

A newspaper article reports on the case of missing children and the 'bloofer lady' (pp. 147–8). All the children who have been missing at night are suffering wounds to their throats.

COMMENTARY

The Victorian era is often associated with an elaborate and luxurious fascination with death and funereal rituals. While the characters most in love with Lucy are given the opportunity to grieve for her loss, Stoker uses some minor characters to punctuate their emotional distress with some mundane, detached observations. The professionals that attend to the dead, and the business of death, add a jarring and cynical humour to the scene. The solicitor's personal pleasure at the legal tidiness of the deaths in the matter of inheritance makes him look foolish and insensitive. Dr Seward remarks on 'the limitations of sympathetic understanding' (p. 139). The undertaker's assistant, whose comments show a macabre blend of professional pride and business acumen, introduces the notion of Lucy's unusual appearance. The appeal of her beauty increases now she is dead, much to the disturbance of those who loved her. It is the first significant sign of the life after death that Lucy will inherit from her vampire lover.

Stoker has not drawn much attention to Lucy's physical attractiveness before this point in the novel. The fact that three young suitors competed for her attention has been the major evidence of her appeal to the opposite sex. Dr Seward is struck by the intense beauty of Lucy several times in this chapter; he notes: 'Every hour seemed to be enhancing her loveliness' (p. 140). His impressions are reinforced by the reactions of Arthur and Van Helsing. They all doubt that she is really dead. Van Helsing has more reason to doubt than the others. The references to Lucy's attractiveness also set the key word 'beautiful' that will be picked up in the reports of 'the bloofer lady' at the end of the chapter.

Dr Seward's response to Van Helsing's outrageous plan to mutilate Lucy's corpse seems surprisingly restrained. His reaction is reported in Van Helsing's dialogue – 'Ah! you a surgeon, and so shocked!' (p. 137) – and in Seward's willingness to trust Van Helsing without much further elaboration. They are conspirators, operating behind Arthur's back. Van Helsing refers in passing to Lucy as '*it*' and by using this term he emphasises that the dead body is no longer Lucy but a thing.

Mina and Jonathan Harker are reintegrated gradually into the narrative. Among the sequence of deaths and funerals, Jonathan's chance recognition of Dracula begins to shock him out of the state of amnesia and provides Mina with a motive to discover the truth of his past. The death of Lucy brings Van Helsing into contact with Mina Harker, and this starts drawing the parts of the narrative together for the participants. Mina's sad lament for Arthur's loss

> **CONTEXT**
>
> Consider the descriptions of Lucy in the light of this observation from the physiognomist Johann Lavater (1741–1801): 'Of the many dead persons I have seen, I have uniformly observed that sixteen, eighteen, or twenty-four hours after death (depending on the disease) they have had a more beautiful form, better defined, more proportionate, harmonized, homogenous, more noble, more exalted than they ever had during life.'

of 'such sweetness' gives a measure of her sympathetic nature, and subtly aligns her with the living (p. 144). Mina never makes much comment on her friend's death. Although she often refers to her later as 'poor dear Lucy' she makes no more developed comment on her feelings or Lucy's nature. Stoker manages to create a distance between the characters, without making Mina seem either indifferent or too sympathetic to Lucy's fate. This maintains the implicit moral contrast between the two women's natures.

CHECK THE FILM

Wes Craven's *Vampire in Brooklyn* (1995) takes the romance of the vampire and sanitises the vampire character with comedy.

Van Helsing's explanation of his strange humour – 'King Laugh' (pp. 145–6) – seems both idiosyncratic and profound. Van Helsing has a lively appreciation of the common impulse to laugh at the most inappropriate moments; he has a sense of the ridiculous and a sense of humour. This compassion for the tragicomical contradictions of the human condition makes him seem sympathetic and avuncular. There is a sense here that his wisdom sets him somewhat apart from the experience of the other characters because he is of an older generation. He speaks of his 'father-heart' and his 'husband-heart' when describing his feelings (p. 145), emphasising his experience of life and the roles he has played in caring for others.

It is Arthur's sentiment in declaring the blood bond between himself and Lucy to be a form of marriage that has sparked Van Helsing's sad humour. Stoker allows Van Helsing to infer two things from this notion. First, that Lucy is a 'polyandrist'; and second, that he is a 'bigamist' (p. 146). Both words convey a sense of unorthodox sexual behaviour. If Lucy, according to Arthur's theory, has 'married' him, she has also 'married' the three other men who gave her their blood. Van Helsing does not elaborate on the fact that Arthur's ignorance of his wife's other 'husbands' places him in the classic position of the cuckold. This is another significant suggestion of promiscuity in Lucy's nature.

The newspaper reports of the 'bloofer lady' (p. 147) as both a threat to children and a children's game neatly combine the way real horrors are transmuted into playfulness through the imagination, and the suggestion that Lucy has risen from the grave. There is another perverse reference to religious beliefs of resurrection here as Lucy assumes the role of Antichrist. The Christ figure is often represented as the saviour of little children. Lucy's first choice of victim unites her with the vampire women at Castle Dracula, whom we saw devouring a small child as an alternative to the 'kisses' they wished to extract from Jonathan Harker (Chapter 3, pp. 33–4).

The phrase the 'bloofer lady' may or may not be an accurate depiction of the accented transformation of the word 'beautiful' in the vernacular speech of children in Hampstead at the time. Stoker certainly relied on research for the other accents he uses and he follows literary and theatrical **conventions** of the time in his depictions of working-class characters.

There is an extraordinary example of intertextuality at work in this incident. Stoker's readership would have been familiar with the works of Charles Dickens and may well have recognised a connection to an episode in *Our Mutual Friend* where a child dies and leaves 'A kiss for the boofer lady.' Whether this is a conscious connection on Stoker's part or evidence of an unconscious influence on his text is not the essential point.

Stoker, in 1897, is mining the same conceptual seam of the child as innocent victim of circumstance as Dickens did three decades earlier. However, there is a marked difference in emphasis. Dickens's child death scenes are sentimental, tear-jerking affairs, and he is ever sympathetic to the parental fear of losing a child. Stoker exploits those fears in *Dracula* for purposes of horror, and does not linger on the death of an individual child. His child characters are incidental to the needs of the plot and play only the role of innocent victim.

Stoker seems careful to represent the children as sexually innocent beings. Although they are aware of her beauty, the highly charged sexuality of the earlier depictions of vampire activity is not an overt part of Lucy's vampire attacks on the children.

CONTEXT

This quote by little Johnny can be found in Chapter 9 of the second book of Dickens's *Our Mutual Friend* (1864–5). Infant mortality was higher in 1865 and Dickens's sentimental idealisation of the dying child must be seen in that context. Stoker's children are not much more than vampire fodder in comparison.

CONTEXT

Intertextuality is a device used by many writers. It is the blending into a text of ideas, references, often actual words, which suggest a connection or parallel between it and other texts. Its purpose – serious, comic, parodic, contrasting, contradictory, and so forth – will depend on the context.

CHAPTER 14

- Mina Harker reads Jonathan Harker's journal.
- Mina meets Van Helsing.
- Jonathan meets Van Helsing.
- Van Helsing asks Dr Seward to believe that Lucy Westenra is responsible for the attacks on the children in Hampstead.

GLOSSARY

151 **verbatim** Latin for an exact transcription or 'word for word' report

156 **physiognomist** a person who believes that features of the human face reveal the truth or moral qualities of character

Mina reads Jonathan Harker's journal, and fears he may be mad. Nevertheless, she decides to transcribe the journal from shorthand to a typewritten manuscript, but does not tell her husband that she has done this. In a letter Van Helsing requests her assistance; she invites him immediately to Exeter. Mina feels guilty that she kept Lucy's sleepwalking a secret, but is glad that she has typed up her own journal, so that Van Helsing might read it.

Van Helsing is described by Mina, who thinks of him immediately as a friend. He tells her of Lucy's diary and asks about the sleepwalking in Whitby. Mina gives him her journal. She cannot resist the joke of handing him the shorthand copy first, then hands over her typewritten version. After reading it, Van Helsing is excited and sings her praises. He enquires about her husband and she describes the incident in London. Van Helsing says she has restored his faith in womanhood. She trusts him with her husband's journal, but does not expect him to believe it. He tells her that he has an open mind, and they agree to meet the following morning.

QUESTION Van Helsing is described as an 'arbitrary' person by some characters and an advocate of open-mindedness by others. What is the significance of this apparent contradiction?

In a letter delivered by hand Van Helsing reassures Mina that her husband's experience was indeed real. Jonathan is transformed by this news, and explains the debilitating effects of uncertainty: 'It was the doubt ... that knocked me over. I felt impotent, and in the dark, and distrustful' (p. 156). Van Helsing asks for more information about the events that took Jonathan to visit Castle Dracula, and Jonathan provides some papers for him to read. As Van Helsing boards the train back to London, he reads the news of the attacks on the children in Hampstead.

Dr Seward resumes his diary, complaining that there is 'no such thing as finality' (p. 157). Van Helsing points out the news of the injured children to Dr Seward, who sees the coincidence of the neck wounds. Van Helsing speaks at length about the mysteries of existence and the limits of human understanding; he talks of the difference between prejudice, mystery, belief and science, and mentions bloodsucking spiders and bats. He also raises the question of immortality. Dr Seward asks him to explain more clearly, and Van Helsing explains the function of faith, saying that he wants Dr Seward 'To believe in things that you cannot' (p. 160). He concludes by announcing that the children have been attacked by Lucy.

COMMENTARY

The description Mina gives of Van Helsing itemises the characteristic features associated in the practice of physiognomy with a dominant and powerful personality of good, honest intent. Although there is much that resembles Jonathan Harker's description of Count Dracula in Chapter 2, the telling detail of contrast is the tenderness she detects in Van Helsing's eyes. Though Van Helsing may be 'stern' his nature is not cruel; Mina comments that she feels, having seen him, that 'he *is* good and kind and of a noble nature' (p. 151).

Van Helsing is impressed by Mina's cleverness in the use of modern methods, and is surprisingly ignorant of shorthand himself. This touch of nineteenth-century modernity defines Mina as a resourceful person and it emphasises the fact that Van Helsing is older, knowing the wisdom of the past better than the fads of the moment. Mina's skills are important to the communication between the major **narrators** of the novel, and her organisational and secretarial skills will be formative in the construction of the narrative as a whole. Mina's minute knowledge of railway timetables fits in with this aspect of her character and will also be of greater significance later on. Van Helsing praises her, this 'clever woman', for giving him hope that 'there are good women still left to make life happy' and 'make good lessons for the children that are to be' (pp. 153–4). This is the first explicit reference to Mina as a possible mother figure, an image that has never been applied to Lucy.

CONTEXT

Shorthand evolved as people tried to solve the problem of recording speech. People, on average, speak about five times quicker than anyone can write. Sir Isaac Pitman presented his phonetic short form of writing in 1837. Although quite established by the end of the nineteenth century, it was superseded by developments in sound-recording devices.

Van Helsing's confidence in the truth of Jonathan Harker's journal is an important validation of Jonathan's experience. It is a moment of restoration for both characters. Jonathan is restored to confidence and manhood by his approval; Van Helsing is restored by this healing act which gives him new strength following his failure to prevent Lucy falling to her destruction. Van Helsing draws his new hope from Mina Harker, and she will come to play a similar inspirational role for all the men.

Van Helsing leads Dr Seward through a consideration of various extraordinary phenomena in the way a teacher might lead a pupil towards a difficult concept. Dr Seward falls easily into the role of pupil trying hard to maintain his status in learning but struggling to keep up with his teacher. Van Helsing challenges him first to explain the cause of Lucy's excessive blood loss. He cannot. Van Helsing does not give him the answer. First, he praises him for being clever and bold, but admonishes him for ignoring important mysteries and being 'too prejudiced' (p. 158). He feels Dr Seward lacks interest beyond the scientific explanations of the world. 'Ah, it is the fault of our science that it wants to explain all; and if it explain not, then it says there is nothing to explain' (pp. 158–9). Van Helsing ascertains that Dr Seward does not believe in 'corporeal transference', 'materialisation', 'astral bodies', and 'reading of thought' (p. 159).

It is significant that Dr Seward rejects these pseudoscientific phenomena but accepts hypnotism to be credible. Van Helsing seems to be asking Dr Seward to take account of phenomena associated with theosophy, a mystical philosophical view popularised in the latter part of the Victorian era. Stoker knew something of this esoteric and allegedly scientific attempt to combine orthodox religious belief with belief in supernatural or paranormal phenomena. The same phenomena appear in other works by Stoker, and his writing draws on diverse influences such as freemasonry, Egyptology and medieval folklore to achieve its occult credentials.

Dr Seward is bewildered by Van Helsing's rhetorical listing of a dozen or so of 'nature's eccentricities and possible impossibilities'. In response to Dr Seward's plea for a clear 'thesis' or basic idea,

CONTEXT

In 1875 the Theosophical Society was founded in New York City by Helena Blavatsky and Henry Steel Olcott.

Van Helsing simply asks him 'To believe in things that you cannot', or in other words to have faith. He goes on to give a definition of faith as 'that which enables us to believe things which we know to be untrue' (p. 160). This definition appears to have been in general circulation at the time as an amusing but childish paradox and it can be found in almost exactly the same form in Mark Twain's *The Tragedy of Pudd'nhead Wilson*, published in 1894. Stoker does not allow Van Helsing to recall the name of the 'American' he 'heard once of', nor the fact that he is a famous and very popular author. As Stoker had known Mark Twain personally for some time, this reference to his friend's recent work seems intended as an **ironic** and humorous little 'aside'.

CHAPTER 15

- Van Helsing and Dr Seward discover Lucy Westenra's tomb is empty.
- They rescue a child from Lucy, the 'bloofer lady'.
- They postpone their attempt to save the undead Lucy in order to involve Arthur, Lord Godalming.
- Arthur reluctantly agrees to go along with the plan.

GLOSSARY

161 **tussock** a small spiky knotted growth of grass

166 **unhallowed** unholy or sacrilegious; a reference to the 'hallowed' or sacred ground of the grave or tomb, and a reminder of the unhallowed grave of the suicide in Chapter 6

Dr Seward is outraged by Van Helsing's suggestions that Lucy is attacking the children. Van Helsing assures him that it can be proved. By night they visit Lucy's tomb and find her coffin empty. Van Helsing is not surprised, but Dr Seward is bewildered and cannot explain the absence of the body. Waiting in the graveyard, Dr Seward sees a white figure approaching and Van Helsing rescues a child, which they leave for the police to find.

They revisit Lucy's tomb during the day. This time Lucy is in her tomb, and Dr Seward is amazed that she looks so healthy and 'more radiantly beautiful than ever' (p. 166). He is still sceptical but cannot explain why her corpse has not begun to decay. Van Helsing reveals that Lucy was bitten by a vampire while in a trance, and Seward starts to think this is the only possible explanation.

CONTEXT

The episode of the two men entering Lucy's tomb is reminiscent of the climactic scene in Shakespeare's *Romeo and Juliet* where the young lovers are finally united in death.

CONTEXT

Dr Van Helsing's **metaphor** of contrast here ('thorny paths … paths of flame') is reminiscent of the religious **imagery** of the *Bhagavadgita*, a sacred text of Hindu scripture, particularly the chapter 'Of the Religion of Knowledge'. This may have been assimilated through Stoker's association with the Theosophical Society, but the imagery is also common in Christian texts, and here is a specific reference to the eternal flames of hell.

Van Helsing intends to destroy the vampire that Lucy has become. He hesitates, however, and suggests it would be better if done by Arthur. They lock Lucy's tomb and depart. Later Van Helsing returns to watch the grave at night and seal it with garlic and a crucifix to prevent Lucy from leaving; in a note he orders Dr Seward to read the Harkers' journals.

Following a 'good night's sleep', Dr Seward thinks Van Helsing is 'unhinged' and vows to 'watch him carefully' (p. 169). He and Van Helsing meet with Quincey Morris and Arthur. Van Helsing asks for their trust, knowing that Dr Seward is not fully convinced. Quincey gives his at once; Arthur agrees, but with reservations. He is amazed by Van Helsing's plan to open the tomb. Van Helsing explains it is necessary in order to save Lucy's soul, announcing passionately and ominously that 'this night our feet must tread in thorny paths; or later, and for ever, the feet you love must walk in paths of flame!' (p. 171). He suggests that Lucy is not dead, prompting Arthur's horror that she has been buried alive. He is deeply offended by the suggestion that Lucy may be in danger of eternal damnation. Van Helsing explains that Lucy is now 'Un-Dead' (p. 171), and reveals that he wants to cut her head off. Arthur is scandalised, but Van Helsing reveals their common bond through his giving 'the blood of my veins' to Lucy and states that he is willing to give his own life on her behalf, if it 'can do her good even now' (p. 172). Arthur is impressed by his sincerity and, though he does not understand, agrees to the plan.

COMMENTARY

This chapter brings the main male characters together and, in establishing their common purpose, explores the notions of friendship, love and duty. Van Helsing is cautious in leading his pupil towards an understanding of the situation, and he is aware that his task of persuading the other two men will be equally difficult. Stoker has created bonds of friendship that place the men under obligation to one another to trust each other and assist each other in return. The younger men are united by past adventures and dangers they have shared, and they have their love of Lucy as a common feeling. Van Helsing is bound to Dr Seward not only as his mentor but because Dr Seward once saved his life. The four men are united as 'blood brothers' in the act of giving their blood to Lucy.

The moment when Dr Seward saved Van Helsing is mentioned in Chapter 9 and, curiously enough, the bond was made by Dr Seward sucking Van Helsing's blood. The link between Van Helsing and his pupil is the exact reverse of the link between the vampires and their master. Dr Seward is inspired by Van Helsing's goodness to remove poison from the blood: a life-giving action. In contrast, Dracula spreads fatal contamination to victims who act without free will; his motives are evil.

The visit to the tomb draws on mythic traditions of visiting the underworld and appeals directly to the Victorian preoccupation with spiritualism, the possibility of communication with the dead. Places of death are powerfully **atmospheric** and have a special totemic significance in the literature of most cultures. The absence of the corpse is the first moment of challenge to Dr Seward's scientific perspective. His attempts at rational explanation are the last moments of his defence of logic. Outside the tomb, Dr Seward fails to see the vampire clearly; Lucy is merely 'something like a white streak' to him (p. 165). Van Helsing is given a small victory here in the rescue of the child. This also allows us to retain some sympathy for Lucy, as she is not depicted in the same terms as the vampire women who, though not seen, have been overheard devouring their small prey in Castle Dracula. Her character is not yet beyond redemption.

It is the discovery of Lucy's 'radiantly beautiful' (p. 166) corpse in the coffin when they return to the tomb later that forces Dr Seward to accept Van Helsing's explanation of her as 'Un-Dead'. Van Helsing's justification of her preserved beauty as an expression of her sweet nature emphasises that Lucy is not like the other vampire women. She became a victim in a 'trance' and that preserves

CONTEXT

Many of Britain's graveyards, if not established in the Victorian era, show the influence of Victorian society's morbid fascination with death. The larger tombs and mausoleums are displays of economic status and class position. The social divide was clearly intended to continue after death. Economic status, as much as geography, determined where a person's remains would be buried.

CONTEXT

Spiritualism, seances and mediums were extremely popular in Victorian England. The craze in attempting to make contact with the dead was seen across all classes but was most vigorously pursued in the wealthier sections of society. Spiritualism was a revival of medieval superstitions under the influence of American social trends in the mid-nineteenth century, and many so-called 'mediums' were later exposed as charlatans. Believers in spiritualism included Sir Arthur Conan Doyle and Elizabeth Barrett Browning; critics included George Eliot and Robert Browning.

something of her innocence. Van Helsing's observation that 'There is no malign there' makes the point clear (p. 167). Dr Seward's feelings of love for Lucy are changed into loathing for the 'being' she has become. He characteristically poses a speculative philosophical question to himself about the nature of love: 'Is it possible that love is all subjective, or all objective?' This is the intellectual expression of his bewilderment. The question seems to arise merely in passing, and it is left unanswered.

Dr Seward's conversion to a belief in vampires is not yet complete, however. After a refreshing night's sleep, he begins to consider seriously that Van Helsing may be responsible for the absence and reappearance of Lucy's corpse. He still believes 'there must be *some* rational explanation of all these mysterious things' (p. 169).

The moment when Van Helsing brings Arthur and Quincey into the work of dealing with Lucy is not, as might be expected at this point in the narrative, a full set-piece explanation of the situation. Dr Seward, Arthur and Quincey listen to Van Helsing with cautious but confused curiosity. Arthur becomes the focus for the reaction of mystified horror as Van Helsing outlines his proposal to mutilate the dead body of the woman they all loved. Arthur is dutifully 'protecting her grave from outrage' (p. 171). Van Helsing appeals to his rank and status as a gentleman in an attempt to gain his trust. His speech is short but effective, and Arthur is 'much affected by it' (p. 172).

Van Helsing's proud assertion that he also has a duty to Lucy and to others is eclipsed by the revelation that he has sacrificed his blood for Lucy. It seems this information shakes Arthur's confident resolution to defend Lucy's grave; but the fact that he shakes Van Helsing's hand averts any suspicion of jealousy against the professor on his part. Arthur seems grateful but his 'broken voice', as he says 'I cannot understand', shows how he is overwhelmed by the nightmarish situation.

Arthur at the end of this chapter is a picture of English steadfastness in the face of adversity. His willingness to endure patiently what he does not understand makes him the epitome of the fortitude of the English aristocracy. Although the other men loved Lucy, and are more or less uncertain about Van Helsing's weird notions, Arthur was her chosen lover. As such, he is seen by the others to have some kind of precedence or prerogative in disposing of her bodily remains. In this the men are reflecting the cultural values of a time when women were still essentially controlled and owned by men, much the same as other items of property. Though the legal status of women in marriage had been reformed through the latter part of the nineteenth century, the notion that the woman surrendered herself and disappeared into the man's identity in marriage was still very strong.

Van Helsing's pragmatism in making Arthur the one to destroy Lucy becomes imbued with a romantic significance. It is the final act of love requiring a **symbolic** act of penetration to finish the relationship. It would be inappropriate for another man to usurp this position.

Stoker uses the men's slow realisation of the dangers they must confront as a device to control and maintain suspense over the next few chapters. He creates a wealth of incidents that will demonstrate again how their misplaced discretion, their mistaken confidence in the extent of human knowledge and their unwitting ignorance will leave them all vulnerable. Their errors will endanger that which they most of all wish to protect. The underlying **theme** that unites these episodes is one of the centrality of faith. If these characters are to succeed, they must overcome their unwillingness to believe in things that challenge any form of rational belief. They must abandon reason to gain hope. Van Helsing's mystical appeal to unreason will gain urgency over the next two chapters as the novel approaches its major turning point.

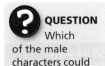

QUESTION
Which of the male characters could be described as 'men of action'?

CONTEXT
In 1882 the Married Women's Property Act gave women rights to ownership of property in marriage.

QUESTION
Are scientists, or science itself, the cause of the failures and disasters in *Dracula*?

CHAPTER 16

GLOSSARY

177 **sexton** the person responsible for supervising the gravedigging and the bell-ringing in a Christian church

- Dr Van Helsing, Dr Seward, Quincey Morris and Arthur, Lord Godalming, go to Lucy Westenra's tomb.
- Van Helsing rescues a second child from the undead Lucy and prevents Arthur becoming her next victim.
- The undead Lucy is destroyed by Arthur; thus her soul is saved.
- Van Helsing proposes they track down Count Dracula and destroy him.

Van Helsing, Dr Seward, Quincey Morris and Arthur, Lord Godalming, go to the graveyard at midnight. They discover Lucy's empty coffin and Quincey and Arthur are amazed. Outside, Van Helsing seals the tomb again, explaining his holy artefacts. The four men then wait.

A white figure approaches carrying a child. Lucy is now a wanton horror with blood on her lips. She advances on Arthur with a 'voluptuous smile' on her lips (p. 175); he goes to her as if 'under a spell' (p. 176). Just in time, Van Helsing saves him with his crucifix, and asks Arthur for his permission to proceed; Arthur agrees. Lucy is allowed to enter her tomb and Van Helsing reseals it and saves the child.

The men, all dressed in black, return to the graveyard the next day and open Lucy's coffin. Van Helsing explains '*nosferatu*' as he prepares to save Lucy's soul and the souls of the children she has attacked (p. 178). Arthur is given the task of releasing her. He stakes her heart and she writhes in her death throes. When he is done, Lucy seems restored to wholesomeness, her face once again 'of unequalled sweetness and purity' (p. 180). Arthur is now allowed to kiss her.

Van Helsing and Dr Seward complete the task by cutting off Lucy's head and filling the mouth with garlic; then Van Helsing explains to the men their shared duty to avenge Lucy and destroy Dracula. They arrange to meet in two days.

COMMENTARY

With the second death of Lucy, this chapter brings to a close the second main phase of the novel. The threat to her soul is averted by the concerted actions of the men who love her. Her first death is a punishment for her misguided ways; her second death is her salvation. It is allowed because she is not like the wholly irredeemable foreign vampire women. This **symbolises** the desire to preserve the innocence of English womanhood from the alien invader.

This second section or phase of the novel has developed the notion of Dracula, primarily, as a threat to the women of Britain. Dracula is an insidious seducer who leads the wayward modern woman into temptation. There is much to suggest that Lucy represents the fate awaiting those with a frivolous approach to life. The next phase of the novel will see that menace directed at Mina Harker, who is presented as more virtuous than beautiful. In attacking her, Dracula will strike at the Victorian ideal of the maternal female. This connects with the notion of ownership of the female identity. Powerful male figures do battle for the woman who will be the source of their next generation. It is a question of whose blood will flow in the future. In presenting an idealised maternity, Stoker is actually expressing the male need for a certain paternity; in other words, children whose paternity is not in doubt because the mother is a virtuous woman. It is consistent with the reactionary view of civilisation or nationhood being something that is 'in the blood'.

Notions of so-called purity of blood and national salvation tend to gain popularity at moments of social uncertainty. At the end of the nineteenth century this was linked to the sense of rapid transformation in social conditions. The modern age brought new influences to bear on conventions, customs and traditions. At the same time, the British Empire, though still strong, was in competition with other empires and under threat. The monarch, Queen Victoria, was elderly and her reign could not last for ever. Stoker's novel is an often decadent expression of these fears of technological advance and loss of heritage.

> **CONTEXT**
>
> In 1887, according to the *Lancet*, there were approximately eighty thousand prostitutes in London, though this may have been an underestimation. Attitudes to prostitution changed in the nineteenth century and the 'oldest profession' came to be regarded as a major social problem. As the population of London was just over two million, the evident scale of the problem can be appreciated.

On one level, the novel is appealing to the national myth of St George and the dragon. Dracula is derived from the Romanian word for dragon. Lucy is easily seen as a damsel in distress, and this role is shared with Mina. Only one of them will survive the encounter with the dragon, though both are saved from his clutches. The role of St George the dragon slayer is taken at different times by Arthur, Van Helsing and Jonathan Harker.

CONTEXT

The Host is the consecrated bread believed by Catholics to be, through the act of transubstantiation, the body of Christ. In Catholic doctrine an indulgence is a relief from worldly punishment granted to those seeking forgiveness for sins committed, not an amnesty in advance for unacceptable behaviour.

Van Helsing's belief in the Roman Catholic religion is revealed here more clearly than by the use of the crucifix in the earlier chapters. In sealing up Lucy's tomb he makes use of the 'Host' brought especially from Amsterdam and permitted to him by 'an Indulgence' (p. 174). Although the others do not share the same religious views, they are 'appalled' by Van Helsing's apparently sacrilegious use of the symbol. The term 'Indulgence' here suggests that Van Helsing has been given permission by some church official of high authority to act in this way. Van Helsing, using a symbol that is, as Dr Seward points out, 'the to him most sacred of things', impresses upon the men his sincerity of purpose (p. 174). It also identifies him as the most religious character, the man with the strongest faith. As he is a Roman Catholic, this is not an insignificant aspect of the religious **themes** of the novel. Stoker, as an Anglo-Irish writer, would have been well aware of the significance for his readership of the tensions between these two branches of Christianity.

CONTEXT

American editions of the text make this more obvious: Lucy's hair is described as 'sunny ripples'. This is an example of how some minor textual discrepancies lend weight to various readings of the novel.

Dr Seward refers, in his description of the scene, to all the elements that make a graveyard by night such a dismal place of horror: 'ghastly white' tombs; gloomy 'funereal' trees that 'rustle so ominously' with boughs that 'creak so mysteriously'; and the woeful 'howling of dogs'. At first he cannot see the 'dim white figure' clearly. A 'dark-haired woman' approaches and is suddenly illuminated by 'a ray of moonlight' (p. 175). It may be a small point, but Stoker even changes the colour of Lucy's hair to emphasise how much she has transformed. In Chapter 12 Dr Seward had admired her 'shiny ripples' of hair (p. 133). This is the only direct description of her appearance in the novel. This change of hair colour also associates Lucy with the vampire women in Castle Dracula, two of whom were dark-haired.

At first Dr Seward does not recognise her. Lucy, to Dr Seward so full of 'sweetness' and 'purity', is now a nightmare figure of 'adamantine, heartless cruelty' and 'voluptuous wantonness' (p. 175). By the light of Van Helsing's lantern they can all see the blood on her lips. Lucy's 'pure, gentle' eyes are now 'unclean and full of hell-fire'. The word 'unclean' will be repeated by Mina Harker later in the novel. Lucy's treatment of the child is 'callous', revealing a 'cold-bloodedness … that wrung a groan from Arthur'. But she seems possessed of a 'languorous, voluptuous grace' as she approaches Arthur, and her voice is 'diabolically sweet' as she entices him into her arms. Van Helsing prevents Arthur from falling under her spell, and Stoker calls forth **imagery** from Greek mythology and several different cultures to describe the 'rage' and 'baffled malice' in Lucy's face (p. 176). Seward's little joke – 'if looks could kill' – does not detract from the impact of the scene.

Dr Seward comments on the fact that they are all wearing black, the colour of mourning and appropriate to funeral rites, when they meet again to return to the graveyard. When they open the tomb, Dr Seward describes how Lucy's 'death-beauty' no longer holds sway over his emotions (p. 177). He is obviously repelled by the 'carnal' thing she has become.

Arthur in his resolute dispatching of 'the foul Thing', hammering the stake into Lucy's heart, is compared to Thor, the Norse god of thunder. Dr Seward sees the writhing and 'wild contortions' of the vampire but his focus of attention is the God-like, courageous and steadfast Arthur. Lord Godalming is, literally, a shining example of manhood amidst the spurting blood. The sexual allusions are not very far from the surface, but Stoker does not dwell on the scene. Arthur's exertions are rewarded with the re-emergence of Lucy's 'unequalled sweetness and purity' on her face (p. 180). Arthur is intensely grateful to Van Helsing for the 'peace' he has been given. This recalls Lucy's deathbed plea to the professor and establishes a sense of closure to this second phase of the novel.

The end of the chapter moves us into the next phase of the novel, with Van Helsing's invitation to the men to join him, and some others, in 'a greater task' (p. 181).

> **CONTEXT**
>
> In Greek mythology Medusa was one of the Gorgons, whose face was so terrible that all who looked at her turned to stone. Her head was a mass of writhing snakes. She was killed by Perseus, who cut off her head.

> **CONTEXT**
>
> In Scandinavian mythology Thor was the god of thunder, the weather and agriculture. His weapon was a hammer, emblematic of the thunderbolt.

GLOSSARY

182 **inquisition** the word means official examination, but it has a specific reference to the suppression of heresy or unorthodox belief in the history of the Roman Catholic Church

189 *ex post facto* Latin phrase meaning 'having retrospective effect' or, more simply, 'afterwards'. Jonathan is explaining why he has assumed Dracula's responsibility for tipping the workers

CONTEXT

The expression 'Honest Indian' is a statement intended to affirm the truth. It seems to have been in use before Mark Twain popularised it in *The Adventures of Tom Sawyer* in 1876. Either Dr Seward is supposedly up to date in his reading of the American author, or his American friend Quincey has had an influence on his expressions.

CHAPTER 17

- Mina Harker transcribes Dr Seward's diary.
- Jonathan Harker discovers the location of Count Dracula's boxes of earth.
- Mina prepares the narrative of diaries, journals and articles.
- She comforts Arthur and Quincey Morris.

Mina Harker arrives in London and is met at the station by Dr Seward; he takes her to his asylum. She has brought her portable typewriter. In his study Mina notices Dr Seward's phonograph, and he explains how he keeps his diary. Mina asks about Lucy's death, and Dr Seward is horrified at the thought of telling Mina how her friend died. He tries to dissuade her from this idea by using the excuse that he has no way of selecting particular passages from his diary, admitting: 'That's quite true, upon my honour. Honest Indian!' (p. 183). She offers to transcribe his recordings. He is reluctant to allow her to do so, and she suggests he read her diary, and that of her husband. He agrees, and they read each other's journals.

Jonathan Harker is in Whitby gathering information. Mina is now convinced there should be no more secrets between the friends. She transcribes more of the diary, copying everything in triplicate. When Jonathan arrives the next morning, they busy themselves 'knitting together' the evidence from the recordings and journals in chronological order (p. 187).

Dr Seward explains how they have discovered Dracula's hiding place; at last they begin to understand the significance of Renfield's violent behaviour. They know it is related to the movements of Count Dracula, but at the moment Renfield seems unusually sane. Jonathan is on the trail of the boxes.

Mina now has all the papers in order. Arthur and Quincey are given a copy of all the assembled documents, and Arthur breaks down in grief. Mina offers him motherly comfort and he pledges himself to her. Quincey remarks on Arthur's need for comfort, and Mina reaches out to him too; Mina, Arthur and Quincey arrive at a new understanding of their relationship to one another.

COMMENTARY

The third phase of the novel begins with the gathering of the group that will commit themselves to the destruction of Dracula. Mina Harker's character is repositioned in the narrative as the woman to be defended by the men, and it is implied that her character is more worthy of that role than Lucy Westenra. Van Helsing describes her to Dr Seward as a 'pearl among women' (p. 181).

This chapter also creates the motive for Mina to begin the organisation of the papers that form the basis of the narrative as a whole. All their records need to be shared in order for them all to arrive at a common understanding of their experience; as Mina points out to Dr Seward: 'We need have no secrets amongst us; working together and with absolute trust, we can surely be stronger than if some of us were in the dark' (p. 185). The reader has been placed, throughout the novel, in the position of one of the intended readers of the history, and given privileged access to their pool of knowledge.

Jonathan Harker re-enters the narrative in vigorous pursuit of information. His journal notes, with a hint of the old sardonic humour that can be seen in the first part of his journal, the not so subtle forms of bribery he uses to secure the knowledge of the location of the boxes belonging to Dracula. He also assists Mina with the ordering of the papers for the records.

Arthur now has a moment of emotional release as he mourns his loss of Lucy in the company of Mina Harker. His appreciation of her 'sweet sympathy' brings her into the limelight previously occupied by Lucy (p. 191). This is confirmed, as she notices herself, when Quincey praises her 'true-hearted kindness' and calls her 'Little girl' – his term of endearment for Lucy (p. 192). She effectively supersedes Lucy as a worthy object to inspire them in their quest. For her part, she is filled with admiration for their courage and friendship.

> **? QUESTION**
> From the middle of the novel onwards the writers of the story are also readers of each other's words. They are now catching up with the reader in their understanding of the plot. What effect does this device have?

CHAPTER 18

GLOSSARY

199 **pabulum** food, meaning the particular form of nourishment an animal needs to maintain life, i.e. for vampires, blood

200 **scions** offshoots or branches on a tree, a word often used to describe the sons of a noble family

200 **coevals** people of the same age group, contemporaries

- Renfield appears to have knowledge of Lucy Westenra's death.
- Dr Van Helsing outlines the greater task facing the men.
- Mina Harker is excluded from the quest for her protection.
- Renfield begs Dr Seward to release him.

Mina asks to see Renfield, and Dr Seward, although anxious he may be dangerous, agrees. Mina is gracious with Renfield, who is contemptuous to Dr Seward but courteous and respectful to her. He explains his madness to her and blesses her.

Van Helsing returns from Amsterdam and retires after dinner to read a copy of the journals. All details are now to be included in the official record. Later that evening the group meet to discuss their actions and the task that lies before them. Van Helsing leads the committee and gives a brief history of Count Dracula and an outline of the characteristic features of a vampire.

They all make a solemn vow to destroy Dracula. Now Van Helsing itemises the weaknesses of a vampire, giving some more historical detail on Dracula. He says they must find and sterilise the boxes; their first task must be to search Carfax and investigate how many boxes remain there. Suddenly the window is shot out by Quincey, who had slipped out of the room. He explains he was shooting at a large bat at the window. Continuing with his plan, Van Helsing informs Mina that she is to be excluded from their quest to protect her from harm.

As Mina retires to her bedroom, the men prepare to head off to Carfax for immediate action. Just as they are about to leave the house, a message arrives from Renfield, who is demanding to see Dr Seward. The four men visit him together, and he begs, in a completely sane manner, to be released immediately, for the good of his soul. When this is refused, he asks that they remember his request.

COMMENTARY

Mina Harker is now acting the role of homemaker. She brings an **archetypal** feminine touch to all the proceedings of the group as they define their task. Van Helsing is extravagant in his praise for her 'man's brain' but 'woman's heart' (p. 195).

All the details given by Van Helsing concerning Dracula are confirmations of things that have been alluded to by the **narrators** in their accounts so far. This elucidation is for the characters' benefit, but it draws together the various strands of myth, legend and history that Stoker has made use of at various points in the story. Van Helsing plays the role of a military strategist marshalling his knowledge of the enemy to define his campaign. The '*nosferatu*' may be strong but they have certain weaknesses which the group can make use of. We learn that Dracula 'is not free' but in some respects is 'more prisoner than … the madman in his cell' (p. 199).

Dr Seward calls his friends Arthur and Quincey 'the boys' (p. 195), a typical note of male bonding in the group, but it does also hint at a willingness to be almost childlike in response to the presence of Mina, who has made his house seem, for the first time, 'like *home*' (p. 193). Renfield's lucid comment on the men is also revealing: 'You gentlemen, who by nationality, by heredity, or by the possession of natural gifts, are fitted to hold your respective places in the moving world', as it is intended to be evidence of Renfield's perspicacity at this point (p. 203). This is the view any sane person of the late Victorian age might be expected to take of these remarkable men.

> **CONTEXT**
>
> The terms 'cult of domesticity' and 'cult of true womanhood' are applied to the Victorian ideals of family life, the woman as homemaker, wife and mother and the woman as expert in the sphere of emotion.

CHAPTER 19

- Dr Van Helsing, Dr Seward, Quincey Morris, Jonathan Harker and Arthur, Lord Godalming, go to Carfax.
- They discover twenty-one boxes have been removed.
- Mina Harker has a disturbing dream.

GLOSSARY

212 **obliquity** a sudden switch in direction or angle. The word can also imply criticism of a mistaken or deviant moral direction

The men make their way to Carfax, Jonathan Harker happy that Mina is not part of the danger. Quincey Morris feels sorry for Renfield, while Dr Seward realises the madman is connected in some way to Count Dracula. Van Helsing gives each man a number of items, including a crucifix, garlic blossoms and a portion of sacred wafer, to protect themselves as they go into the house. Jonathan, who knows the place from working on its plans, leads the way to the chapel. It stinks, the smell seeming to Jonathan to be 'composed of all the ills of mortality … as though corruption had become itself corrupt' (p. 208).

They check the boxes and discover twenty-one are missing. Something moves in the shadows, and suddenly thousands of rats appear. Arthur alone is 'prepared for such an emergency', and he calls in some dogs to deal with the rats while they continue with their search. As they return home, they hear Renfield making a noise. Jonathan finds Mina asleep but pale; when he wakes her the next day, she looks at him 'with a sort of blank terror, as one looks who has been waked out of a bad dream' (p. 211).

Van Helsing rouses Dr Seward the next day and asks to see Renfield, who is very rude to him. Van Helsing and Seward discuss memory and its relationship with thought. Quincey and Arthur go off in search of the boxes of earth.

Mina Harker has mixed feelings about being excluded from the dangers faced by the men. She keeps a diary for Jonathan, writing about how all their best intentions to shield her from anxiety have produced exactly the opposite result. She recalls a strange fog and Renfield's struggles, but does not share her memory of dreaming about a strange 'livid white face' with red eyes with anyone (p. 215). After visiting Renfield, she takes drugs from Dr Seward to help her sleep.

COMMENTARY

This chapter is full of the most startling **ironies**. Despite her own previous acknowledgement that secrecy has not been a good idea, Mina does not share her strange dreams with anyone. This could be explained by the reaction she has to being excluded from the manly activity, but it does seem odd that her ability to make connections fails her at this point. Is this evidence of the Count's influence already at work? The fact that no one notices her unusually pale complexion as an ominous sign after Lucy's experience is most odd.

Mina recognises that her dream has similarities with her husband's accounts of the vampires in his journal: 'Suddenly the horror burst upon me that it was thus that Jonathan had seen those awful women growing into reality' (p. 215); yet still she does not question whether her dream is, in fact, real. The 'white mist' and the 'livid white face bending ... out of the mist' are, of course, no dream.

The greatest irony is, of course, the fact that by excluding her and giving her drugs to sleep soundly, the men are making her easy prey for Dracula. Their decision not to release Renfield is another crucial mistake, as the Count will use Renfield to gain access to the house and to Mina. The chapter ends on her prophetic and anxious realisation that taking the sleeping draught provided by Dr Seward might not be such a good idea after all; that she 'may have been foolish in thus depriving myself of the power of waking' (p. 216).

CHAPTER 20

- All the boxes are located.
- Jonathan Harker uses Arthur's title and influence as Lord Godalming to gain information about Count Dracula's house in Piccadilly, London.
- Dr Seward notes that Renfield wants the life but not the souls of those he devours.
- Renfield is injured.

GLOSSARY

224 **cerebration** literally 'brain action', derived from Latin. It refers particularly to unconscious activity in the brain

CONTEXT

Stoker gives his **narrators** an amused indulgence of the working-class characters' tendency to 'thirst'. Victorian attitudes were not so typically relaxed about the evils of the drink. The temperance movement, inspired by the Nonconformist religion, succeeded in establishing the Licensing Act of 1872, which fixed the closing hours of public houses at 11 p.m. for the country and midnight for London.

Jonathan Harker traces more drunken workmen and locates the other boxes. He tracks down an estate agent who, impressed by Jonathan's mention of Lord Godalming, gives him the information they need.

Jonathan notices how pale and unwell Mina looks, and feels guilty for keeping things from her. Van Helsing is now very confident, and they discuss plans to enter the Count's house in Piccadilly.

In an interview with Dr Seward, Renfield speaks of being afraid of being burdened with the souls of those he has eaten. The doctor questions him but does not understand Renfield's answers. The idea of the soul is a torment to Renfield; 'Life is all' he wants (p. 223). Pondering the significance of all Renfield has told him, Dr Seward realises with horror that Dracula has been with Renfield. He tells Van Helsing his suspicion. Later on, while Van Helsing is away at the British Museum consulting old books, Renfield is injured.

COMMENTARY

Stoker again has some fun depicting the differences between the language used by characters of different classes and the problems of communication that arise as a result. The trick here is worked by the device of misunderstood pronunciation and phonetic spelling. Jonathan Harker is so caught up in his sleuthing that he is unaware of the dangerous turn of events for Mina. In his defence, it might be said that Jonathan had not seen Lucy's degeneration, so could not be expected to recognise the symptoms in Mina; but he has had some experience by now to put him on his guard, and he has read his wife's account of Lucy's behaviour in Whitby.

The relationship between the Harkers is somewhat strained at this point as neither deals honestly with the feelings they both experience following Mina's exclusion from the tasks of the group. Despite frequently breaking down in tears when alone, Mina makes a 'gallant effort to be bright and cheerful' in company (p. 221); Jonathan, meanwhile, feels guilty.

Dr Seward's deduction regarding Renfield's association with the Count is another example of information not fully understood until too late. His feeling that 'there is some new scheme of terror afoot!' is another warning not heeded (p. 226). These signs are understood by the reader, who fully anticipates the disaster that is about to befall the group.

The chapter concludes with the bloody attack on Renfield, an alarming indication of more trouble that turns out to be a diversion from the real danger.

CHAPTER 21

- Renfield reveals he invited Count Dracula into the asylum.
- Dracula is discovered forcing Mina Harker to drink his blood.
- Mina describes Dracula's plan to use her to punish those who would dare to oppose him.
- Renfield dies.

> **GLOSSARY**
>
> 230 **suffusion** the way a liquid spreads across or through a surface
>
> 230 **trephine** a more refined version of the trepan or surgical saw for cutting into the bone of the skull
>
> 230 **haemorrhage** dangerous loss of blood due to a ruptured blood vessel

Renfield is found, horribly injured, lying in a 'glittering pool' of his own blood (p. 228). Van Helsing is fetched and quickly takes charge. Renfield is examined, and Van Helsing and Dr Seward decide to operate on him. Arthur and Quincey arrive, the former roused by the attendant calling Van Helsing.

Renfield speaks of a dream, yet he knows it was a 'grim reality' (p. 231). He explains how he was unable to speak before, and that it was he who invited Dracula into the asylum. He knew Dracula had been to see Mina by the way he smelt and he knew that she was not the same when he saw her again; her blood 'had all seemed to have run out'. He says Dracula is 'taking the life out of her' (p. 233).

CONTEXT

Franz Anton
Mesmer
(1734–1815), an
Austrian physician,
began
experimenting
with what he
called 'animal
magnetism' in the
early 1770s as a
cure for mental
illness. His
methods involved
the inducement of
trance-like states
but depended for
any success on the
susceptibility of
his patients.
Mesmerism, the
forerunner of
hypnosis, was
discredited. At
least part of the
criticism of
Mesmer was the
possibility that
his 'treatment'
removed women's
sexual inhibitions.

Van Helsing leads the men to rescue Mina. They break into
the Harkers' room and see Count Dracula forcing her to drink
blood from a cut on his breast. Jonathan lies on the bed, 'breathing
heavily as though in a stupor' (p. 234). Dracula escapes. Mina has
a 'thin open wound' on her neck and feels 'unclean' (p. 236); she
has to restrain Jonathan from rushing out to look for Dracula.
The Count has been in the study and destroyed all the copies of the
journals and diaries; fortunately one copy remains in the safe.
Renfield is dead.

Mina describes being attacked by Dracula. Dracula plans to use her
to destroy those who would thwart his plans; he tells her that she,
'their best beloved one', is to him now 'flesh of my flesh; blood of
my blood; kin of my kin … and shall be later on my companion and
my helper' (p. 239).

COMMENTARY

A gruesome physical operation leads into Renfield's account of
his dealings with Count Dracula. It reminds us that Dr Seward
and Van Helsing are medical surgeons as well as natural
philosophers. Renfield's description of the persuasion used by
the vampire is a combination of semi-religious awe and jealousy.
There is no overt suggestion of the sexual energy encountered in
the other moments of hypnotic vampirism. Renfield is tempted by
the prospect of a seemingly unlimited supply of lives in return for
'worship' (p. 232). His submission to this is retained in the use of
the capitalised pronoun whenever he speaks of Dracula. This is
conventionally reserved for the Christian deity or God, and the
implication of devil worship would not have been overlooked by
Stoker's readership.

Renfield is not motivated to resist Dracula until he realises that
Mina is among 'the pale people'; his remark 'I like them with lots
of blood in them' is a chilling reminder of his insane obsession.
But the realisation that Dracula is attacking Mina has an effect on
him. As he says, 'it made me mad to know that He had been taking
the life out of her'. Renfield's insane strength is no match for the
Count's terrible mesmeric power: 'I saw His eyes. They burned

into me and my strength became like water' (p. 233). Renfield is crushed and obviously near death, but the narrative is no longer concerned with the madman, whose death is reported by Arthur shortly afterwards.

Stoker has his heroes leap into action realising they 'know the worst now' (p. 233). They burst through the Harkers' door and discover the tableau of horror that is Dracula in action. This is the only moment in the novel where Dracula is seen clearly by the **narrator** and the reader in the act of attacking his victim. This is not the expected 'kiss' on the neck or the act of bloodsucking, however. The roles are reversed and there is an element of force in the scene that suggests rape rather than seduction. This is an important distinction for the portrayal of Mina as innocent victim. Dracula is restraining her and 'forcing her face down on his bosom'. The description of the scene is curiously restrained and Dr Seward's comparison of this to 'a child forcing a kitten's nose into a saucer of milk to compel it to drink' seems grotesquely inappropriate (p. 234). The jarring note of this impression conveys both the startling horror of the scene and his inability to comprehend it.

Jonathan Harker has been reduced to helplessness by Dracula's hypnotic powers and is distraught at the sight of blood on his wife's nightdress. Mina's cry of 'Unclean, unclean!' (p. 236) evokes the biblical stories of lepers who had to warn others of their infectious state. Jonathan is immediately cast into the role of the righteous Christian by comforting her at this point.

The end of this chapter moves from Mina's state of guilty desperation to Jonathan's state of shock, apparent physically in his 'grey look' and 'whitening hair' (p. 240). He seems to cut a miserable figure here – a warning of what might happen to those who leave their wives at the mercy of such powerful temptation.

See **Text 3** of **Extended commentaries** for further discussion of part of this chapter.

 CHECK THE FILM
Hammer Films' 1958 *Dracula* (titled *Horror of Dracula* in America), with Christopher Lee as Dracula, has the vampire showing his fangs for the first time, and the sexuality of the role is more fully suggested. This was Lee's first of many portrayals of the Count on screen, and his elegant Dracula was a chilling sexual predator.

CHAPTER 22

GLOSSARY

245 **exigency** the immediate needs of the moment

- Mina Harker rejoins the group.
- Count Dracula's lair at Carfax is destroyed.
- The men break into the Piccadilly house and discover one box is missing.

Jonathan Harker writes that Mina has told him their faith in God is being tested. Renfield's death will be explained away as 'misadventure' without further investigation (p. 241).

Mina is now recalled to the group; there will be no more secrets. Van Helsing suggests it is possible she may be a threat to others; Mina declares that she is ready to kill herself 'if I find in myself ... a sign of harm to any that I love' (p. 241). But Van Helsing warns her it is vital she remains alive; else with her death she will become 'the quick Un-Dead ... even as he is' (p. 242). Mina resumes her role as secretary to the group, while Van Helsing takes command and gives them all their orders. Dracula's lairs must be sterilised. Jonathan is impatient to begin, even if it means having to break into the Count's house in Piccadilly. Van Helsing, however, suggests using a locksmith to gain access, and they decide that discretion and deception are necessary for their cause.

Before the men leave, Van Helsing takes steps to ensure that Mina is well guarded. He touches her forehead with a sacred wafer and she gives a 'fearful scream' as it 'burned into the flesh' (p. 246). The significance of this is not lost on any of them, and she repeats her earlier cry of 'Unclean! Unclean!' (p. 247).

The men destroy the Carfax lair before going on to London. Arthur uses his title to convince a locksmith to open the door of the Piccadilly house. It stinks 'vilely' inside, and there are only eight boxes. One is missing. Quincey and Arthur depart for the Count's other London locations to destroy his lairs.

COMMENTARY

Mina is the motive now for the group's urgent action against Dracula. Whereas before they were motivated by a sense of duty to protect unknown others from their unsuspected nemesis, Mina provides a concrete **symbol** of what the men are fighting for. The purpose that may be attributed to Arthur or Dr Seward of wanting to avenge Lucy's memory is now superseded by the desperate need to save Mina. The counter-attack phase of the novel is now moving into action. The men are on the trail of the vampire.

Mina acquires a 'mark of shame' on her forehead that links her, in more ways than one, with Dracula (p. 247). This 'devil's mark', though caused by a holy symbol, reminds us of the notion of the Antichrist and is an outward symbol of her possession. Dracula also has a mark on his forehead, given by Jonathan Harker in his failed assault in the chapel of Castle Dracula. It is a way of subtly suggesting that there is, perhaps, not such a great difference between hero and villain after all. This paves the way for Mina to show pity for her enemy later on. Forgiving the monster that has destroyed her friend and her own happiness elevates Mina almost to the rank of sainthood.

Van Helsing becomes an openly religious guide to them all in this moment of crisis. Jonathan comments that Van Helsing speaks 'so gravely that I could not help feeling that he was in some way inspired … stating things outside himself' (p. 247). Having been the sage, Van Helsing now becomes the priest as they all kneel in front of him, kissing his hand, praying for guidance and swearing loyalty to each other.

The chapter finishes, as so often, with a set-up for the next chapter's events. The men prepare to ambush Count Dracula in his house in Piccadilly.

 CHECK THE NET

In 2005, David Nixon, the artistic director of the Northern Ballet Theatre, brought a brand new interpretation of *Dracula* to the stage. To read a review, go to **www.thestage. co.uk** and search for 'Dracula'.

- The men ambush Count Dracula in his Piccadilly house.
- Dracula escapes.
- Dr Van Helsing hypnotises Mina Harker and she reveals that Dracula is escaping on a ship.

GLOSSARY

254 **Kukri knife** a curved knife, broader towards the point of the blade, used by the Gurkhas of Nepal

In the Count's Piccadilly house Jonathan Harker, Dr Van Helsing and Dr Seward await the return of the other men. Van Helsing reminds them of Dracula's immortality and how he can afford to 'wait and go slow' (p. 252). The vampire is developing and gaining strength slowly. A telegram from Mina alerts them to Dracula's imminent arrival. It is uncertain who will appear first: Quincey and Arthur; or Dracula.

Fortunately it is Quincey and Arthur who are the first to arrive. Quincey takes charge and deploys the men ready for Dracula's appearance. When he comes, Dracula leaps into the room and fights them. Just in time, Dr Seward brandishes a crucifix at him, and Dracula escapes through the window. As he escapes, Dracula promises to make them all his slaves. Nevertheless, Van Helsing is sure that Dracula is afraid.

The four men return to Mina. Again she feels pity for Dracula, and Harker is shocked. She points out she may need such pity herself in the not too distant future. Her words make them all very emotional, and they all weep. After the Harkers have retired to bed, Quincey, Dr Seward and Arthur take it in turns to stand guard outside their room.

CONTEXT

Hypnotism, a term coined in 1841 by the Scottish surgeon James Braid, was the subject of much scientific enquiry at the end of the nineteenth century. Stage hypnotists were very popular in Victorian and Edwardian theatres.

In the early hours of the morning, Mina asks to be hypnotised by Van Helsing. She feels that before dawn breaks she 'can speak, and speak freely' (p. 259). Under a trance, Mina reveals that Dracula is now on board a ship. She wonders why they cannot just allow Dracula to leave, but Van Helsing points out that he can merely wait for her to die, and 'Time is now to be dreaded – since once he put that mark upon your throat' (p. 262).

COMMENTARY

Another of Van Helsing's similarities to Count Dracula emerges in this chapter. He has the power to hypnotise women, though in his case it is an act of healing in the service of their honourable quest. Van Helsing informs the other men of Dracula's quest for advancement and power: 'Soldier, statesman, and alchemist ... He had a mighty brain ... and there was no branch of knowledge of his time that he did not essay' (p. 251).

Van Helsing considers the success of Dracula's experiment in moving to London and sets out the consequences of their failure. Dracula will go on to be 'the father or furtherer of a new order of beings, whose road must lead through Death, not Life' (p. 251). In other words, not just Western civilisation but all of humanity are threatened by Dracula. Here again we see fears of an insidious alien menace. One alien begets many and, before anyone realises, the whole of society is enslaved.

The second face-to-face encounter with Dracula as vampire is a failed ambush. Dracula leaps into the room ready for the attack, and Dr Seward compares him to those dangerous predators the panther and the lion as the men close in on him. Dr Seward, brandishing the crucifix and holding the holy wafer, feels 'a mighty power' flying along his arm (p. 255). The man of science seems to have taken refuge beneath the sign of the cross.

Dracula escapes but is given a second villain's monologue, addressing the reader in his own voice this time, to vent his awful threats against his pursuers: 'My revenge is just begun! ... time is on my side' (p. 255). He promises they shall all become his 'creatures'; the 'girls that you all love are mine already'. The aristocratic contempt Dracula expressed for the peasantry in Transylvania is now directed at the educated metropolitan middle class. Yet Van Helsing detects fear in Dracula and is excited by this

CHECK THE BOOK

George du Maurier's novel *Trilby* (1894) is about a young woman manipulated by a hypnotist named Svengali. Under his guidance she becomes a famous singer, but his power over her is so great that when he dies her voice collapses.

CHECK THE BOOK

A similar concept underpins *The War of the Worlds* by H. G. Wells, published the year after *Dracula*. This **theme** of alien menace also recurs in much twentieth-century science fiction.

CONTEXT

Dracula has an unusually pragmatic attitude to money, as seen when he stoops to retrieve the cash he has lost when ambushed by the men. His hoarded wealth is part of the image of villainy.

GLOSSARY

267 **the old knights of the Cross** a reference to the leaders of the medieval military invasions of the East known in Europe as the Crusades to the Holy Land which began at the end of the eleventh century and continued for about two hundred and fifty years

first sign that they are gaining some ground against their enemy. But he acknowledges that Dracula has the advantage of longevity. They cannot rest content with merely driving the alien out of the country, as is revealed to them through Mina's hypnotic trance; they must pursue their enemy and destroy him utterly, even if it means following him 'to the jaws of Hell!' (p. 262). On this note the third phase of the novel is concluded. The last phase, the chase, is about to begin.

CHAPTER 24

- The men prepare to chase Dracula across Europe.
- Mina Harker appears to be changing.
- Plans are drawn up.
- Mina and Jonathan Harker are aware their relationship has altered.

Van Helsing explains the nature of the battle they have begun. Jonathan is almost sceptical again, yet cannot doubt the 'red scar' on Mina's forehead or the connection with Dracula it represents (p. 263). Mina records what they have discovered about Dracula's departure. There is only one ship headed for the Black Sea on the next tide, bound for Varna. The sudden fog which comes to surround the ship is evidence of Dracula being on board.

Van Helsing talks of Dracula's special origins and how he represents a threat to all mankind. Dr Seward reluctantly discusses with him how far they should trust Mina. She is changing, 'the characteristics of the vampire coming in her face' (p. 269). They fear that Dracula will make use of her connection to him to 'compel her mind' to reveal their plans to him, and they decide she must be excluded from the group's plans. Mina, however, withdraws herself from their discussions herself.

They prepare for the hunt, and Quincey gathers conventional weapons to guard against any physical dangers they might face. Mina demands that Jonathan make a promise 'holily in God's hearing' that he will not tell her any of their intended plans for their campaign against Dracula; upon his swearing she feels a barrier has come down between them (p. 271). Later Mina insists on being part of the hunt, telling Van Helsing that it will be safer for all of them if she goes with them. She points out that Dracula will compel her to follow in any case. Van Helsing agrees. They write their wills before departing.

COMMENTARY

Van Helsing is shown to be a man of the late nineteenth century, willing to embrace all its wonders, in using the phonograph to record a message for Jonathan Harker.

Van Helsing's long description of Count Dracula's special powers and aptitudes shows he has the wisdom to respect his enemy. As he says, Dracula is an exceptional vampire: 'With this one, all the forces of nature that are occult and deep and strong must have worked together in some wondrous way' (p. 266). He attributes the Count's successful invasion of London to the particular qualities of the land where he lived as 'Un-Dead' for so long, and to his own great qualities. It is the first hint that Dracula is somehow a tragic figure, a great man who, through some flaw, falls to evil. Van Helsing admires his 'iron nerve … subtle brain … braver heart, than any man' but concludes his considerations of Dracula with the observation that 'in this enlightened age, when men believe not even what they see, the doubting of wise men would be his greatest strength' (p. 267).

The chapter ends with them all poised to set off in pursuit across Europe. Jonathan confides a note of uncertain hope in his diary, knowing he is having to hide his feelings from his wife. This is a marked contrast to the journal he wrote setting off on his last journey across the continent.

> **CONTEXT**
>
> Quincey Morris suggests they include Winchesters in their armament. The original Winchester rifle was famous for its lever-action breech mechanism that allowed the rifleman to fire a number of shots before having to reload. It was commonly known as 'the gun that won the West'.

> **CONTEXT**
>
> Dracula travels on board the *Czarina Catherine*. This is an allusion to Catherine the Great of Russia (1729–96), whose reputation as a powerful despot was as notorious as her alleged promiscuity.

GLOSSARY

28 **Transcendentalism** philosophical term associated with metaphysics; in the nineteenth century it referred mainly to a belief in things beyond human senses

281 **will-o'-the-wisp** also known as jack-o'-lantern: anything that misleads and vanishes, often associated with marshland or mists and frequently referred to as a strange light. The 'blue flame' in Chapter 1 is a similar phenomenon

285 **egotistical** self-obsessed

CONTEXT

Baptism is the initiation ceremony in the Christian Church that involves ceremonial washing and cleansing.

CHAPTER 25

- The men vow to kill Mina Harker should it be necessary.
- Their planned ambush of the Count in Varna is thwarted by Dracula's change of destination.
- Van Helsing and Dr Seward suspect Mina of unconsciously revealing to Dracula their whereabouts.
- Van Helsing uses Mina's connection to Dracula to their benefit.

Dr Seward notices how Mina is most free at sunset and sunrise. She requests to see all the men just before sunset, and again asks them to promise to kill her if she is ever so changed that she is beyond redemption. Individually they give their promise: Quincey, Van Helsing, Arthur, Dr Seward, and finally Jonathan. Mina asks Van Helsing to promise that it will be Jonathan who dispatches her. She warns that the time may come upon them suddenly. At his wife's request, Jonathan reads aloud the burial service for the dead and they all take comfort from the prayers.

In Varna, Mina is hypnotised again, and they wait for Dracula's ship for a week. Van Helsing is concerned about Mina's lethargy, and a mysterious fog appears around the port. There is no news, until they hear that Dracula's ship has arrived in Galatz. Dracula has escaped their ambush for a second time.

Van Helsing and Dr Seward become more suspicious of Mina, and Van Helsing fears that Dracula used Mina while in her trance to discover their whereabouts and plans. Van Helsing and Mina realise that Dracula is going home. Mina is not yet entirely his slave and he is intent on escape; consequently they can use her to get to him. The 'terrible baptism of blood' Dracula has given her can finally be turned to their advantage; Mina is now 'free to go to him in spirit' by Van Helsing's 'volition and not by his [Dracula's]' (p. 286).

COMMENTARY

This chapter is dominated by foreboding. A morbid sense of doom is set by the discussion of Mina's death, and this mood reaches a funereal climax in their pledges to destroy her. Their vows are sealed in the solemnity of prayers for the dead. This is a particularly macabre scene.

The pace of the narrative has stalled in the anticlimax of the characters lying in wait for Dracula again. Van Helsing seems to be the only one who fears that Dracula may be escaping. It seems odd that Van Helsing, having earlier itemised it in the powers of the vampire, does not recognise the sudden fog as a sign of Dracula's presence. They are still being wrong-footed by the Count.

The shock of Dracula's escape is registered in different ways, but the men who avenged Lucy's death seem momentarily paralysed. The responsibility to respond actively is fulfilled at this point by the Harkers, who, between them, have the determination and the knowledge to set the group back on the right track. Van Helsing calls Mina 'Wonderful woman!' but he is anxious about the connection she has with Dracula (p. 282).

Over a lengthy discussion of the 'predestinate' inclination of the criminal to rely on habit in times of crisis and put self-preservation above all other considerations, Mina is taught by Van Helsing to reason out how she is not entirely under Dracula's control as might be expected. Having made use of her to bypass their trap, Dracula is no longer interested in her. Van Helsing surreptitiously takes her pulse during their conversation and seems pleased: 'Seventy-two only; and in all this excitement. I have hope' (p. 285).

 CHECK THE FILM
Stephen Norrington's *Blade* (1998) takes this notion of the scientific approach to vampirism to its illogical conclusion – setting up a vampire to destroy other vampires – and is relevant to a discussion of the **metaphors** of infection and invasion. The strapline describing the vampire protagonist, played by Wesley Snipes, reads: 'The power of an immortal. The soul of a human. The heart of a hero.'

CHAPTER 26

- They travel further towards Galatz and Dracula.
- Mina Harker makes some vital connections.
- The group divides into three pairs, to attack from different directions.
- All are now hot in pursuit of Dracula.

Van Helsing hypnotises Mina again. As she describes a port, they know Dracula is once again on dry land. As they travel to Galatz, it becomes harder to hypnotise Mina, and her evidence is confusing. They trace the captain of the *Czarina Catherine*, who tells the tale of his lucky voyage. They track the boxes and the trail of murder that leads to Dracula's loyal gypsies.

The men discuss taking Mina into their confidence again, and Jonathan Harker is released from his vow. As Mina types up recent journal entries to keep the record up to date she deduces that Dracula is making his way home on the water, and there are only two possible routes that Dracula can follow. The group is called together, and they decide to divide into three pairs: Dr Seward and Quincey, Arthur and Jonathan, Van Helsing and Mina. Jonathan fears for Mina's safety but knows they are all in the hands of God.

The men buy the resources they need for the last stage of the hunt. They are all armed, even Mina, although she 'cannot carry one arm that the rest do; the scar on my forehead forbids that' (p. 297) – in other words she is no longer pure enough to carry a crucifix. Arthur and Jonathan go by boat; Dr Seward and Quincey travel on horseback; Mina and Van Helsing begin their journey by train.

Darkness falls. Harker and Arthur travel up the river and are told of a large boat ahead moving quickly. Dr Seward and Quincey travel by road; there are signs that snow will come soon.

CHECK THE BOOK

Stoker's detailed research notes for *Dracula* are included in the anthology *Vampyres: Lord Byron to Count Dracula*, edited by Christopher Frayling (1991).

Dr Seward knows that Arthur's boat is in difficulty and they seem to be making frustratingly slow progress. Mina is now travelling in a carriage with Van Helsing. She prays and writes of her love for her husband.

COMMENTARY

Mina's connection with Dracula does not yield as much information about the Count's movements as Van Helsing had hoped. The closer they come to Castle Dracula, the harder it is for Van Helsing to hypnotise her successfully.

The second ship's captain, Donelson, has a Scottish accent as a theatrical touch of character, as his main function is to provide plot **exposition** for the landing of Dracula in his homeland. As the trail goes cold – quite literally coming to a dead end – it is Mina who thinks through the problem and comes up with a solution. In compiling the historical record, Mina has gained a wealth of detailed knowledge which she summarises for the group, and the reader, in presenting her ideas. Her conclusion that the Count must choose one of two routes home puts the group back on track. Van Helsing calls her 'our teacher' (p. 294).

Mina is left marvelling at the inevitability of women's love for men 'so earnest, and so true, and so brave'. She also has discovered 'the wonderful power of money!' (p. 296). Arthur and Quincey are rich and 'willing to spend it so freely', and for that she is thankful. Her husband is aware of the 'wild adventure' they have begun (p. 298). Between the two of them, the notion that they are 'in the hands of God' is repeated three times.

The closing lines of the chapter express Mina's devotion to her husband in a committed and serious manner. She knows she is risking her own life, and more, as they approach the castle, but her thoughts are with her husband.

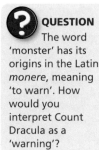

QUESTION
The word 'monster' has its origins in the Latin *monere*, meaning 'to warn'. How would you interpret Count Dracula as a 'warning'?

GLOSSARY

304 **unavailingness** lacking purpose or ability to carry out tasks

307 **leiter-waggon** described in Chapter 1: 'the ordinary peasant's cart, with its long, snake-like vertebra' (p. 8)

308 **clarion** trumpet or horn which produces a shrill high note

312 **centaur** mythological creature, half-man, half-horse

CHAPTER 27

- Dr Van Helsing and Mina Harker approach Castle Dracula.
- The three vampire women visit them during the night but cannot enter their protective holy circle.
- Van Helsing destroys Dracula's lair and the three women.
- The three groups converge on Dracula for the final battle.
- Dracula is destroyed, but Quincey Morris dies.

Mina and Van Helsing are travelling quickly through the countryside where Jonathan Harker's journal began. Van Helsing hypnotises Mina, and her response suggests Dracula is still travelling on the river. Mina still feels 'unclean' and worries for the safety of her husband. As they draw near the castle, it becomes more difficult to hypnotise her. She sleeps more heavily, and no longer keeps up with her writing; so Van Helsing takes over the record-keeping.

He senses a new guiding power in Mina, who seems to know exactly where they are. She says her husband's journal is the source of her knowledge of the terrain. Mina sleeps deeply during the day, so deeply that Van Helsing cannot wake her. After sunset, however, she is wide awake, and she watches the professor sleeping. Now he can no longer hypnotise her at all. They both sleep during the day as they approach the castle.

At night Mina is awake, and Van Helsing creates a ring of holy protection around her. The three women vampires arrive from Dracula's castle. Mina warns Van Helsing that she is not the one in danger from these women, who tempt him as they previously did Jonathan with their 'bright hard eyes' and 'voluptuous lips', and call to Mina to join them: 'Come, sister. Come to us' (p. 306). In the daylight Van Helsing prepares to enter Castle Dracula.

There is a brief switch in scene as Jonathan Harker and Dr Seward writing in their journals explain their slow progress in catching Dracula. Dr Seward is aware he may be riding to his death.

Van Helsing goes to the castle; there he destroys the vampire women in the chapel and lays a sacred wafer in Dracula's tomb. As he leaves, he fixes the castle entrance to prevent Dracula entering. When he returns to Mina, they find a hiding place near Castle Dracula and await the arrival of Jonathan. Van Helsing spots Count Dracula's cart approaching, and he again places Mina inside a holy circle. The gypsies driving Dracula's cart are racing for the sunset; two pairs of riders are speeding towards them from different directions.

Snow falls and the sun starts to set. Only Van Helsing and Mina know how close these separate groups in the chase really are to one another. They watch the chase converging.

The sun is nearly set as the men advance. The gypsies defend themselves in a disorganised and chaotic manner, and Jonathan forces his way through and drags the large chest to the ground. Quincey Morris, wounded as he follows, helps Jonathan force the lid open. As the gypsies are held at gunpoint, Dracula's red eyes gleam with hatred. Just in time, Jonathan cuts his throat and Quincey stakes him through the heart. Count Dracula immediately crumbles to dust. Mina is glad to see the look of peace on Dracula's face before his body vanishes.

Mina is released from the curse of the mark on her forehead as Quincey dies, secure in the knowledge that he has not died in vain.

COMMENTARY

There are several reminders of the beginning of the novel in its conclusion. Mina's wistful descriptions of the landscape recall her husband's nervous journal entries. Van Helsing's fears for his sanity, and the fact that he almost falls under the hypnotic spell of the vampire women as he goes about his 'butcher work' (p. 309), also echo the beginning of the novel. Where Jonathan Harker failed in the chapel at Castle Dracula, Van Helsing succeeds. Although the old man relies on his religious **symbols**, the younger generation also put their trust in more mundane powers. Among the wolves, the gypsies and the snow, their knives and guns are put to good use.

 CHECK THE FILM

The Vampire Lovers, a 1970 Hammer film directed by Roy Ward Baker and starring Peter Cushing and Ingrid Pitt, is a loose retelling of Joseph Sheridan Le Fanu's 'Carmilla'. The film was considered somewhat daring at the time of its release on account of its explicit lesbianism and portrayal of female dominance.

QUESTION
Reading *Dracula* as a monstrous representation of 'the other', the excluded or the oppressed, may give us a perspective to sympathise with the Count. Why is Mina so glad to see 'a look of peace' on Dracula's face in his final moment?

Mina's reaction to the Count's death is the most significant part of the conclusion. Dracula dies at the moment the sun sets, just as he thinks he has secured his 'triumph' over his pursuers. His expression changes from hatred to triumph to 'a look of peace' as he crumbles to dust and nothingness (p. 314). Mina is glad for that peace, and this gladness suggests both her merciful and sympathetic nature. The larger suggestion is that even a vampire, and a 'King-Vampire' too, can be forgiven. She is saved by his destruction, but it is important the act has benefits for others beyond her own salvation.

Stoker has held off the denouement of the novel over several chapters. The end is now approaching and the reader is conscious of that imminent resolution. Mina and Van Helsing effectively give the reader a grandstand view of the last stage of the chase. The final battle, the confrontation with the monster, is something of an anticlimax after the long build-up. Jonathan Harker and Quincey Morris together dispose of the cart's dangerous cargo. It is appropriate that Jonathan, the husband of the threatened woman and the first to meet the vampire, and Quincey, the American man of action, should be the ones to deliver the death blows. For Arthur to wield the stake and hammer again would invite comparisons with the previous moment with Lucy; Dr Seward lacks the resolution of the other two. And, in a way, it is fitting that the American is heroically sacrificed to the cause, as is required. The struggle against evil must be won at great cost to establish the significance of the victory.

CONTEXT
Given that America pursued an isolationist path in foreign affairs over the subsequent period and did not commit troops to combat in Europe during the First World War until 1917, this image of the old country being rescued by the new seems somewhat hopeful.

It also suggests, at an **allegorical** level, that the strength of the rising American nation will serve England in resisting the foreign invaders. The English characters survive to remember Quincey with honour, as befits an ally and a worthy equal. But whether *Dracula* is read as an allegory of some desired 'special relationship' between English-speaking cultures or not, the triumph of hope is the key note struck by Stoker in this ending. Quincey, the man of the moment, dies 'with a smile and in silence' (p. 314), achieving another form of peaceful resolution to the last phase of the novel.

NOTE

- It is seven years later.
- Mina and Jonathan Harker have a son named Quincey.
- There is no proof of this tale but their notes.

Jonathan writes of the time that has passed since the events previously described. They now have a son named Quincey. He also is christened in memory of the other members of the 'little band of men' (p. 315). They will tell him of the brave men he is named after and the whole of the story in years to come.

The Harkers have returned to Transylvania, where they find it difficult to believe that such things could have possibly ever happened. The documentary record will hardly convince anyone to believe such a tale.

Arthur and Dr Seward have both married and all are happy. Van Helsing speaks of how young Quincey will some day know how much his mother was loved by the men whose names he bears.

COMMENTARY

The last image of the novel is of Van Helsing, with the child on his knee in the manner of an avuncular grandfather, predicting the future and extolling the virtues of the beloved Mina Harker. Van Helsing represents the power of philosophy and wisdom faithfully pursued and righteously applied in the noble defence of the innocent and vulnerable. The child represents both innocence and the future, secured by the wise and courageous actions of the men. Van Helsing is confident the child will come to understand what sacrifices they made and how they were inspired by the love of a good woman. This gives a sense of moral obligation that future generations should be taught to understand the past, acknowledge their heritage and realise the proper role of the woman: to be worthy of men's love. This vision of womanhood is represented by the mother, 'brave and gallant' Mina, wholly redeemed of the contamination forced upon her.

 CHECK THE BOOK
David J. Skal in *Hollywood Gothic: The Tangled Web of Dracula from Novel to Stage to Screen* (1990) examines the struggles to develop *Dracula* into film and stage productions. Florence Stoker's battle with Friedrich Wilhelm Murnau over the literary rights of her husband's book and her opposition to the 1922 film *Nosferatu* are described in great detail.

? QUESTION
A vampire is nothing more than a bugbear or a bogeyman; to what extent is *Dracula* more than a tale of imaginary terror told to frighten naughty children?

Quincey is eulogised as the hero who laid down his life to save Mina. He was a solid, dependable and straightforward man. But the other main victim is not so easily reconciled with a respectable image of suffering or sacrifice. Lucy Westenra is not mentioned in this summing up of the novel by Jonathan Harker. An indirect reference is implied in the happy fact that neither of her erstwhile lovers is desperate for her memory, as they have married other women. Stoker allows Jonathan to draw a discreet veil over the loss of 'poor Lucy'. After all, Mina is the real 'New Woman' of the late nineteenth century, isn't she? And wasn't it her typewriter that created the pages of the story?

EXTENDED COMMENTARIES

TEXT 1 – CHAPTER 3, PAGES 32–5

From '*Later: the Morning of 16 May*' to 'I sank down unconscious.'

There is a conscious act of defiance in Jonathan Harker's choice to sleep elsewhere in the castle. He comments on the 'pleasure' of disobedience but knows that it is not so much his own strength of character but his tiredness, and sleep itself, that has provided him with the 'obstinacy' to defy the Count (p. 32). It is a little act of rebellion that precipitates a moment of crisis. Jonathan lulls the reader into sharing his own false sense of security as he recounts how he 'composed' himself for sleep amidst the dusty reminders of 'old ladies', their 'sweet lives' and 'gentle breasts'. His description of imaginary women being sad for their 'menfolk away in the midst of remorseless wars' romanticises his situation and also conjures an image of his fiancée in that position. We are reminded of the hopeful, if complacent, traveller at the start of the novel as he waits for sleep gazing at the 'lovely view' (p. 32).

Jonathan hopes that his 'startlingly real' experience was – but fears it could not be – 'all sleep' (p. 32). The moment of waking is not given; he leaps into his memory with the short sentence 'I was not alone'. The mood of the reverie is broken instantly.

Stoker uses the previously established motif of disturbed or uneasy sleep to evoke a titillating moment of seduction that takes Jonathan to the brink of ecstasy. He seems to recognise these women; he is aware that they are at least his social equal if not his superior, for they are 'ladies by their dress and manner' (p. 33). He describes them simply. They are dark and fair, with their eyes and teeth being compared to vivid precious stones. One has eyes like 'pale sapphires' and 'great, wavy masses of golden hair'. All three have teeth 'like pearls'. He emphasises their mouths by immediately juxtaposing this with the 'ruby of their voluptuous lips'.

Jonathan's feelings are in conflict as he is 'uneasy' to be in a situation which combines 'longing' with 'deadly fear' (p. 33). He acknowledges a 'wicked, burning desire' in his heart, and it is he who first mentions the word 'kiss'. His account has the shocked **tone** of a guilty confession, as he is aware that this desire is a betrayal of his fiancée, Mina. Though many commentators interpret this episode as an instance of typically Victorian fear of sexuality, it is not at all clear that Jonathan is afraid of the sexual side of this experience. His reluctant acknowledgement of seduction is bound up with a sense of personal failure and disgrace. He knows that his failure to resist the amorous charms of these 'ladies' is an outrageous departure from conventional morality. When the women speak of 'kisses for us all', they are voicing and teasing his desire. Their laughter, described again in luxurious terms – 'silvery' – is inhuman but musical: 'like the intolerable, tingling sweetness of water-glasses when played on by a cunning hand' (p. 33). This lengthy simile combines the vocabulary of torture, pleasure and fiendishness.

The women seem to be egging one another on to do something they perhaps should not. Jonathan recalls agony and delight as he furtively glances under his eyelashes at the women. One of the women, the striking fair-haired aristocrat with blue eyes, approaches him and he tremulously describes the effect of her breath on his senses: 'tingling through the nerves' (p. 33). It is an intimate detail that arouses expectations of further physical contact.

 CHECK THE NET

The images of the women here recall the paintings of the Pre-Raphaelites. Find out more about these images and the Pre-Raphaelite Brotherhood online at **www.pre-raphaelitesociety.org**

He can smell blood on her breath: a disgusting image that leads into the next moment as he sees how the woman is gloating over him. The word 'voluptuousness' repeats the sense of wanton abandonment to pleasure that he craves, and he finds the woman's animal behaviour 'both thrilling and repulsive'. This depiction of a predatory female is couched in terms that might be used to describe a dog slavering over a bone, her tongue 'churning' as she licks her teeth and lips.

CHECK THE BOOK

For a subtle appreciation of the complexities of Victorian sexuality and social behaviour see *The Making of Victorian Sexuality* by Michael Mason (1994).

Stoker is alluding to the established connection between vampires and wolves here for dramatic effect, but it can be interpreted as a product of a deeper cultural fear of female sexuality embedded in the mores of a patriarchal society. Essentially, here we have refined aristocratic ladies behaving like common prostitutes, all available and enthusiastic participants in the highly sexual act of kissing a man's neck. The masochistic nature of Jonathan Harker's submission to the women is excused with the rather flimsy alibi of his supposition that it might all be a dream. His humiliation is complete when his moment of consummation, the penetration, is denied by the arrival of the Count: 'This man belongs to me!' (p. 34).

Jonathan's account continues in the next chapter, but it is worth noting the pause created by the break for a new chapter. Harker's loss of consciousness is a kind of theatrical or **metaphorical** 'blackout' that allows the scene to be shifted to another time and place. It provides the climax to the episode for the reader, a climax quite literally denied to the participants in the seduction.

Stoker metaphorically depicts human sexuality as a threat to civilised society, an insidious contagion and yet an undeniable pleasure. His characters encounter their sexuality at the edge of consciousness in circumstances of reduced responsibility. This enables Stoker to allow the morally dubious characters to be destroyed by the consequences of their desires and the morally virtuous to be absolved of any blame after they survive their ordeal. The connection of sexual fulfilment and a lingering death is a definitive characteristic of Stoker's use of the vampire **archetype**.

TEXT 2 – CHAPTER 8, PAGES 75–8

From '*Same day, 11 o'clock p.m.*' to 'the reflex of the dawn is high and far over the sea …'

Mina Murray's journal begins Chapter 8 on a weary but satisfied note. Her plans to exhaust Lucy with exercise have been realised. An interesting paradox is given voice when Mina relates the encounter with the 'dear cows': 'we forgot everything, except, of course, personal fear' (p. 75). It implies that fear can have a positive and restorative power. It would be quite easy to over-interpret this silly incident of two young women being startled by some harmless animals, but it is a poignant contrast to the real fears and horrors that are yet to come.

Mina's attitudes are clearly shown when she considers the 'New Woman' and declares: 'Men are more tolerant, bless them!' She clearly associates female emancipation with intolerance and disapproval of healthy 'appetites'. This is immediately contrasted with the tolerance she has to display to a young clergyman who, insensitive to their fatigue, outstays his welcome at supper. Her thoughts on role reversal in marriage, with the 'New Woman' doing the 'proposing', are rather more ambiguous. Is her comment 'a nice job' sarcastic or something more positive? The fact that she finds 'some consolation in that' is not necessarily proof that Mina disapproves of the female usurping the traditional male role. Stoker sets up the mood of happiness and weary contentment, tempered by Mina's thoughts of her fiancé, as a precursor to the change that will follow.

The record of the narrative is maintained with Mina's rather lame excuse: 'No sleep now, so I may as well write' (p. 75). This seems somewhat unconvincing for a character motivated by an ambition to be a 'lady journalist'. Her account of the 'adventure' is more enthusiastic than the preamble suggests. Stoker has to establish the credibility of the moment of authorship in each of his documents and sometimes the reader begins to feel that invention is being somewhat strained. A clearer example of this might be the moment

CONTEXT

The term 'New Woman' was first used in the early 1890s and was used to describe late nineteenth-century writings tackling issues of social change for women. These issues included the desire for better educational and employment opportunities for women. New Woman authors also attacked sexual double standards, and questioned the traditional attitudes towards marriage and motherhood.

of Lucy's fatal encounter with Dracula (Chapter 11). A character with remarkably little previous evidence of presence of mind or inclination to write is suddenly, at the moment of greatest peril, seized by the urge to record events.

Mina's account of the event gives the word 'fear' its full weight again. She senses the absence of her friend as an 'emptiness' before she knows for certain Lucy has gone (p. 75). As she realises that her complacent notion that Lucy could not have left the building 'only in her nightdress' is incorrect, Mina is gripped by a 'vague, over-mastering fear' (p. 76).

Lucy's semi-naked excursion to the graveyard is a barely concealed erotic adventure that once again makes a connection between sex and death. This incident enacts the commonplace dream of being naked in public; such dreams are viewed as a fearful response to the revelation of true personal identity. This is the substance of Mina's concern to prevent a scandal. Lucy's social reputation would be destroyed if she were caught wandering the streets in her nightgown; it could possibly jeopardise her marriage. We are told in passing that it is an hour past midnight as Mina begins her search for Lucy, with 'not a soul in sight'. This is the first hint that Mina is already too late to save Lucy.

Mina's unspoken concern is that this is no mere dream but may be indeed the revelation of Lucy's true identity. Stoker allows Lucy the alibi that she is unaware of her actions, exactly the same caveat given to Jonathan Harker when he submits to the vampire women in Chapter 3.

Though Stoker clearly wants us to understand that Lucy has some character flaw that leads to her fall from grace, she is also depicted as a figure of pity: the foolish virgin. She is a 'snowy white' figure in the distance, which emphasises her virginity and her status as a bride-to-be. White is the colour of purity and also surrender. The darkness, Dracula, is a **metaphorical** shadow over her chastity. The dress **symbolises** her wedding to Dracula, just as the letting of her blood symbolises her loss of virginity.

CONTEXT

A popular 1880s guide to social etiquette contained the following advice: 'Although in England ladies enjoy far greater liberty of movement in public places than is permitted in Continental society, it is not considered proper for unmarried ladies to frequent promenades and the principal thoroughfares, thronged with business-men and pleasure-seekers, unless under befitting escort.' With such defined codes of behaviour, how much more scandalous could the story of Lucy's nocturnal adventure become when 'distorted' as Mina fears?

Lucy's erratic breathing – 'long, heavy gasps' (p. 77) – suggests sexual arousal, possibly even orgasmic ecstasy, and Mina innocently does not recognise the state she is in. Lucy hides her neck, suggesting perhaps a consciousness of shame. Is Lucy merely responding to the pain of the wound or moaning with pleasure at the memory of her dark lover? The telltale marks on the neck, the typical sign of early sexual experimentation in the adolescent, do not mean anything to Mina. The two women are clearly delineated here. Lucy is a sexualised being and Mina is not. Mina's physical modesty, in stark contrast, does not allow her to walk through the streets barefoot. She can endure the pain of walking barefoot, but must conceal the appearance of her naked flesh.

Another of Stoker's **themes**, concealment and the consequences of secrecy, appears at the end of this passage as Mina is made an accomplice in concealing Lucy's adventure. Mina 'thought it wiser to do so' for the sake of Lucy's 'reputation' and 'her mother's health' (p. 78). Mina's fear that 'such a story might become distorted' is doubly **ironic**; her telling of the story distorts the situation that the reader understands only too clearly.

TEXT 3 – CHAPTER 21, PAGES 238–40

From 'The poor, dear lady shivered' to 'the great round of its daily course.'

In this passage, Mina is given the time to describe from her point of view the event interrupted by the men. The technique of embedded or multilayered narrative is used to great effect here. The event is recorded by Dr Seward, who allows Mina to take over the role of **narrator**. Her narrative is framed within his narrative perspective. Stoker takes this a stage further by allowing Mina to voice Dracula's perspective also. It is the only time in the novel when Dracula, though speaking through another character, directly addresses the reader, placing the reader in the position of the character being addressed. Dracula's vengeful and cruel mockery of their attempt to oppose him, given in the form of a villain's monologue, is intensely **melodramatic**. It is the only scene where the threat posed by Dracula is realised in full view of the reader and the characters involved. It is the moment when the bogeyman finally steps out from the shadows.

CONTEXT

William Acton, a Victorian expert on venereal disease, summed up the typical attitude to female sexuality of that period: 'As a general rule, a modest woman seldom desires any sexual gratification for herself.' His book *The Functions and Disorders of the Reproductive Organs* (1857) gave the view that the wife should merely submit to the husband for the sake of a harmonious and stable relationship.

CONTEXT

Melodrama was a term originally used to describe a stage presentation that featured songs or orchestral accompaniment. As these became a truly popular form of theatrical entertainment in the nineteenth century, the levels of audience participation were highly enthusiastic. Moralising and sensational adventures such as *Fifteen Years of a Drunken's Life* by Douglas Jerrold (1828) gave noble-hearted working-class types the chance to get the upper hand over the bourgeois villains who so lecherously pursued honest young Englishwomen. As a dramatic form, it never enjoyed the credibility of the high tragedy it copied. Some see melodrama living on in television soap operas.

Mina's description of Dracula is definitive: 'a tall, thin man, all in black' (p. 239). In those last three words Stoker has inadvertently provided costume instructions, if not the casting requirements, for every subsequent cinematic representation of the Count, and a blueprint for all those who have since imitated Dracula's iconic style of dress. Mina's view of his 'waxen face' and 'sharp white teeth' makes Dracula a figure of death and danger. His 'parted red lips' are an invitation to the feast and a repulsive indication of eagerness on his part. Mina finds herself 'paralysed', 'appalled' and 'bewildered' in his presence.

Dracula's selfish exploitation of others is couched in the most luxurious of terms and counterpointed by the most delicate of fastidious quibbles. His comment before he places 'his reeking lips' on Mina's throat is pure theatrical camp: 'a little refreshment to reward my exertions' (p. 239). Linguistically it is appropriate to the archaic form of English Dracula has learnt from books. He describes her as his 'bountiful wine-press'. The act of drinking Dracula's blood directly from his body, seeing the blood 'spurt out' then being forced to 'suffocate or swallow', is a clear parody of a sexual act (p. 240). The emphasis on her mouth, as she tries to remove the 'pollution' from her lips, reinforces this reference to oral stimulation. Wrapped up in this little scene are notions of ravishment, domination, humiliation and submission. Mina admits that, 'strangely enough', she 'did not want to hinder him' (p. 239), a fact that brings her dangerously close to being a willing victim just like Lucy.

This is the only moment in the novel where Dracula is depicted openly engaged in an act of bloodletting; it is his own blood that is spilt and it is the link that leads to his destruction. The moment of her forced submission to Dracula's will establishes the telepathic or hypnotic connection that will prove invaluable to the men's campaign against the Count. Although Mina must obey Dracula's very thought – 'When my brain says "Come!" to you, you shall cross land or sea to do my bidding' (p. 240) – she will not, in the end, be summoned to his purposes. Mina, however, is driven to question herself and her 'fate', and the bewildered bitterness of her question, 'What have I done to deserve such a fate', is one of her lowest moments in the novel. It is not in her nature to dwell in self-pity, and though she vindicates herself as someone who has 'tried to walk in meekness and righteousness', it is her prayer for 'mercy' and 'pity' for others that shows the depth of her beliefs and convictions at this point. Mina is a stalwart believer who does not at any point waver in her faith in God or in her dutiful adherence to the principles that guide her actions.

The narrative is resumed again by Dr Seward at the end of the chapter, who concludes with a sombre and dreadful note that shows how 'the morning light' does not necessarily make things look better. Jonathan Harker's appearance is almost deathly grim as the shock of his wife's distressing condition takes its toll on him. His 'grey look' and 'whitening hair' make him seem prematurely aged and physically weakened (p. 240). The language here is dreary and the syntax of the last sentence has an almost Shakespearian ring to it. Seward's notion that there can be 'no more miserable house' in the entire world is a muted, downbeat ending to this flurry of sordid excitement.

CONTEXT

It is an ancient myth that hair turns white overnight in response to shocks. Hair can turn white, but it would take about two weeks for any white hair to show. Stoker incorporates the superstition for dramatic effect.

CONTEXT

In particular the language recalls the end of Shakespeare's *Romeo and Juliet*: 'A glooming peace this morning with it brings: / The sun for sorrow will not show his head' (V.3.305–6).

PART THREE

CRITICAL APPROACHES

? QUESTION

QUESTION
Character development is a crucial aspect of any narrative. Which characters are permitted to develop the most in *Dracula* and in what ways? What constraints or limits are imposed upon character development by the style of the narrative?

CHARACTERISATION

Stoker gives sparing detail in his description of the main characters. There is little to form a picture of the men or the women beyond their status, their opinions and their actions. Physical appearances are noted mainly by the characters who take an interest in physiognomy, a popular pseudoscience of the earlier part of the nineteenth century. The details they select for comment prejudicially associate certain features with good or bad moral traits. Each **narrator** tends to be preoccupied with interpreting their own sensations or reporting events. The pace of the narrative is rarely held up by descriptive passages that illustrate a character or define a location. Stoker relies on certain key words and occasional personal foibles to anchor the personalities that appear in this fantasy in the reader's imagination. Sometimes this understated approach can make a reader feel a particular phrase or expression is being overworked, but it generally serves his narrative purposes quite effectively.

The characters are noted here in order of their relative contribution to the forms of the narrative structure.

DR JOHN SEWARD

Known to his friends as Jack, this character carries the main burden of the narrative. He is an ambitious member of the medical profession, specialising in the treatment of insanity. His name is of some significance: Seward can be interpreted as guardian of the sea or of victory. A commander of the English army of the same name features in Shakespeare's *Macbeth* (Siward). It suggests that this character might be expected to fill the role of defender of the realm. It is also an allusion to the tradition of British dominance as a naval and maritime power. But Dr Seward hardly seems the warrior type. His main role in the novel is to provide a sounding board for Van Helsing's explanations and arguments.

Dr Seward is introduced by Lucy as her first unsuccessful suitor: 'a poor fellow … all broken-hearted' (Chapter 5, p. 49). Her report of his 'strong jaw and … good forehead' is confirmed in Mina's impression of him later: 'a man of noble nature' (Chapter 17, p. 184), 'good and thoughtful' (p. 186). His own first words are not so engaging: 'Ebb tide … Cannot eat, cannot rest' (Chapter 5, p. 52); he is the picture of a man lacking spirit, complaining of an 'empty feeling'. His 'whole life ended' following Lucy's rejection, he is 'hopeless', a lacklustre sort of man (Chapter 6, p. 61), and has to find solace in work, in particular his study of Renfield. His unrequited love for Lucy presents him some 'little difficulty which not even medical science or custom can bridge over' when his friend asks for his advice (Chapter 9, p. 93).

Having failed to win Lucy's love, Seward fails to protect her from Dracula. He seems to be offering the reader some kind of warning about the perils of neglecting the proper duties of a man. He is identified with the modern aspects of society in the novel. He records his diary on a phonograph 'where the romance of my life is told' (Chapter 13, p. 147). As a man of science, he is unable to protect Lucy or comprehend what is happening to her. A misdirected telegram means he is not around to help when she is attacked. He is 'so bewildered' (Chapter 12, p. 125), and like Jonathan Harker he fears for his sanity: 'I am beginning to wonder if my long habit of life amongst the insane is beginning to tell upon my own brain' (Chapter 11, p. 112). His reaction to the imminent death of Lucy is sombre and depressing. He is 'sick of the world and all in it' (Chapter 12, p. 132).

Although he is observant of detail and possesses a great range of knowledge, Seward often mistakes or doubts the evidence of his senses. He is trusting and mistakes the maid's avaricious purpose for devotion to her dead mistress (Chapter 13, p. 138). He only belatedly discovers the real significance of Renfield's madness, and though he rightly suspects that the Count and Renfield are in contact, he is as wrong in keeping Renfield in the asylum as he is wrong in keeping Mina out of the hunt for the Count. He has very traditional views about 'men of the world' and women in general (Chapter 19, p. 213). He speaks of being careful not to frighten Mina Harker, who is probably much more resilient in her nature than Seward.

> **CONTEXT**
>
> Dr Seward fulfils much the same function as Dr Watson in the Sherlock Holmes series by Sir Arthur Conan Doyle. The companion or 'sidekick' who fails to grasp the point is a familiar sight in many detective novels. As the expert explains to the companion, we are invited to feel superior to the companion in our understanding of the situation.

QUESTION Dr Seward is a medical scientist investigating the workings of the human mind. How far do the Gothic traditions of 'madness' or the fear of insanity apply to this character?

Dr Seward seems to see life as a 'puzzle' and he is frustrated to discover that his scientific view of the world does not give him the answers he needs. His philosophy develops to embrace the notion that 'nature works on such a hopeful basis that we believe against ourselves that things will be as they ought to be, not as we should know that they will be' (Chapter 25, p. 281). His 'sheer anger' at Van Helsing's revelation that Lucy is not truly dead makes him, not unreasonably, fear that his old mentor can no longer be trusted (Chapter 15, p. 161). He uses, surprisingly perhaps, some rather unscientific expressions as he considers whether Van Helsing is mad, 'unhinged' or 'off his head' (p. 169). It is symptomatic of his 'old doubting frame of mind' that he has no great trust in physiognomy (p. 170). As he greets Jonathan Harker, he wonders 'if one can judge from his face' that Jonathan is 'uncommonly clever' and 'full of energy' (Chapter 17, p. 187).

Dr Seward habitually suppresses his emotions. He excuses his typically male lack of comforting vocabulary by affirming the value of non-verbal communication in his inarticulate attempts to share Arthur's grief over Lucy: 'A grip of the hand, the tightening of an arm over the shoulder ... are expressions of sympathy dear to a man's heart' (Chapter 13, p. 140). But he weeps, as they all do, for Mina and Jonathan Harker's desperate anguish. Seward is the first to see Dracula with Mina, and his 'heart seemed to stand still' (Chapter 21, p. 234).

Seward does know, however, what it is to be a hunter. He speaks of the 'savage delight' he felt at the prospect of killing Lucy the vampire (Chapter 16, p. 175). As he approaches the final battle to defeat Dracula he senses a 'strange excitement in the air' (Chapter 27, p. 307).

Despite all his failures and uncertainties, Dr Seward is such a large part of this narrative because he learns to trust Van Helsing and his older wisdom or metaphysics. His acceptance of the solemn pledge to defend Mina sees him fulfilling his role as guardian. Dr Seward, who began as broken-hearted, is restored through his journey to faith and to duty. He ends, reportedly, as a 'happily married' man (Note, p. 315).

JONATHAN HARKER

The Harkers, as a couple, represent heroic and virtuous conduct in the face of terrible temptation. Mina is a model of feminine virtue and Jonathan a classic example of masculine youth growing to mature responsibility. This up-and-coming young member of the legal profession narrates about a third of the novel and is the immediate link to Count Dracula. He diligently prepares for his 'dealing with a noble' in Transylvania (Chapter 1, p. 3). He introduces himself as a recently qualified solicitor, and his naive observations on the foreign realm are replaced by neurotic anxiety as he tries to reconcile his experiences and beliefs. His role in this romantic adventure is that of lover, husband and hero. The balance of his participation in the narrative prevents him being seen as the hero of the novel, the rescuer, the singular St George defeating the dragon. He takes his place in the line-up of masculine types defending their women.

Jonathan Harker, a 'quiet, business-like gentleman' (Chapter 17, p. 187), is the male character whose masculine integrity is most directly challenged. No other character recognises the sexuality of the desires aroused by the temptations on offer. His voice relates the most openly erotic episode in the novel. This test of his character leaves him full of guilty self-doubt, as he is only reprieved from indulging his urges by his captor. He does reject the 'awful women' and gives the explicit comparison between the extremes of femininity depicted in the novel: 'Faugh! Mina is a woman, and there is nought in common. They are devils of the Pit!' (Chapter 4, p. 46).

His position as a prisoner about to be devoured by evil women recalls many old fairy tales. His masculinity or 'manly' credentials are reaffirmed in his brave climb down to the Count's window to explore – 'At the worst it can only be death' (Chapter 4, p. 40) – and his almost suicidal mountaineering escape down the 'steep and high' precipice of the castle, where 'At its foot a man may sleep – as a man' (p. 46).

After the first phase of the novel, Jonathan does not return to the fray directly until the men begin the counter-attack. His inability to face the reality of his memories leaves him in a weakened and nervous state. He appears to be less certain of himself and of his role

CHECK THE FILM

For a film in a more light-hearted vein, try Mel Brooks's *Dracula: Dead and Loving It* (1995). Although the comedy is not to everyone's taste, Mel Brooks makes fun of the major cinematic adaptations in this over-the-top parody.

as a man. 'If only I knew!' is his refrain (Chapter 13, p. 143). 'It was the doubt as to the reality of the whole thing that knocked me over. I felt impotent, and in the dark, and distrustful' (Chapter 14, p. 156). But at the same time, he is endowed with wealth and position through an inheritance supplied by a benefactor. These benefits are a sign of the respect he has earned in his own right and they confirm others' faith in his virtuous nature.

Jonathan regains his vigorous demeanour when his faith in his own manhood is restored. Van Helsing makes him 'a new man' (Chapter 14, p. 156). The significance of the notion of regeneration or rebirth has obvious resonances with the Christian faith. All his fear, 'even of the Count', is banished by the knowledge that all he'd written in his diary was the truth.

CHECK THE NET

Search a comprehensive online encyclopedia such as **www.en.wikipedia. org** to discover more about vampire beliefs and the vampire in history and literature.

In the third phase of the novel his legal knowledge is useful in the pursuit of the vampire, but he is tormented by the fact that his wife has been seduced by Dracula. Dr Seward describes his 'studied calmness' and how this act of self-control strains his 'nervous power to the utmost' (Chapter 21, p. 237). Yet despite his 'haggard' appearance, 'he is like a living flame' (Chapter 23, p. 251), and his friends and his wife have to restrain his righteous anger and eager thirst for revenge. Jonathan speaks of being willing to sell his soul to see Dracula in hell and also later says he would become a vampire himself to be with Mina if all else should fail. But he allows himself to be guided by the wise counsel of Van Helsing and by the compassion of his wife.

Harker is finally able to gain his revenge upon his jailer and his wife's seducer. The 'sweep and flash of Jonathan's great knife' (the phallic **imagery** here is easy to detect) reasserts his masculine superiority over the foreign usurper (Chapter 27, p. 314). The ending shows how he is rewarded for his defence of social stability, but leaves him with a nagging sense of insecurity that the story, his story, will not believed. As usual, he allows Van Helsing to have the last word, suggesting that he believes it is enough that his son will one day know the essential truth that love of a good woman was his inspiration and his salvation.

MINA HARKER (NÉE MURRAY)

Bram Stoker, introducing the story in a 1901 edition, described Mina as 'a woman of character', though he also chose to refer to her as Harker's wife rather than dignify her with her own name. This may be nothing more than the common convention of his time, but it does signify an attitude that is clearly conveyed in the novel as a whole. Mina sees herself at all times as a dutiful subordinate partner in her relationship to Jonathan Harker and as a role model for her less reliable friend Lucy.

As an ideal of femininity, Mina is shown to be resourceful, caring and meticulously organised. Seen through the eyes of the male characters, Mina is utterly beyond reproach and apparently flawless. Van Helsing, the epitome of wisdom, acknowledges her outstanding intellectual qualities first of all: 'so clever woman' (Chapter 14, p. 152), 'wonderful Madam Mina … pearl among women!' (Chapter 17, p. 181). His respect for her as a woman is expressed as an appreciation of her intelligence. His comment that Mina has male qualities in her thinking, praising her for possessing 'a brain that a man should have were he much gifted', is to a twenty-first-century reader an example of outdated gender-biased assumptions (Chapter 18, p. 195).

At the end of the nineteenth century, if women dared to venture into activities considered men's affairs they were derided. Men in positions of power prevented women from demonstrating their potential to equal or exceed the achievements of men. In many fields of intellectual endeavour – for example medicine; the arts, particularly writing; or business – women were presenting a challenge to dominant attitudes, but it was difficult for women to secure education or training in any discipline. In such conditions, most individuals who succeeded were, by necessity, privileged, determined or exceptionally able. Mina possesses those qualities but does not present a challenge to the dominant position of men. She is worthy of respect and unthreatening. Van Helsing raises her almost to the status of 'honorary man' in praising her capacity for thought, going as far as to describe her as 'our teacher' at a

> **? QUESTION**
> Mina Harker could be seen as a **symbolic** representation of the Irish nation with Count Dracula representing the political 'threat' of separation from the British Empire. What might the other characters represent?

later stage (Chapter 26, p. 294). This is a turning point in her development as a character.

Mina is employed as a teacher in the first phase of the novel and acts as a companion to the younger Lucy in the second phase before becoming the wife of a solicitor. In the third phase of the novel she acts as nurse and comforter to her husband. Her ambitions to write are channelled into serving as a secretary to the men. She is portrayed in the role of homemaker, adding a softening touch to Dr Seward's forbidding establishment; he comments on her 'sweetly pretty' but sad presence in his asylum (Chapter 17, p. 184). She becomes an innocent victim of Dracula's vengeance. In the last phase of the novel, Mina watches the 'brave men' battling on her behalf and is only allowed to participate in the quest under certain restrictions. Her exceptional nature as a 'brave and gallant woman' enables the transformation from young teacher to ideal **personification** of Victorian motherhood.

In the moment of the novel's climax, the battle between the men and Dracula, Mina's love for her husband is almost religious in its intensity: 'her eyes were pure and glowed with fervour' (Chapter 27, p. 309). There is a sense of moral destiny in the journey this character makes through the novel. Van Helsing remarks: 'God fashioned her for a purpose' (Chapter 18, p. 195). It could also be said that Stoker has fashioned her for a purpose, to depict the ideal of harmonious family life that must be defended from all harm. In many ways, Mina is a version of Britannia, the regal female symbol of national identity, whose moral virtues place men under the obligation to 'dare much for her sake' (Note, p. 315).

This vision of femininity and masculinity in a reciprocal relationship, each bound by duty and honour to romantic self-sacrifice, is a profoundly conservative outlook. Mina's character, in expressing her love for Jonathan and her emotional life in general, is passive and restrained. Her love is a pure emotion without obvious physical reality. She and her husband are rewarded with a child, a son and heir, but the propriety of their relationship is preserved through its privacy.

CHECK THE FILM

Francis Ford Coppola's *Bram Stoker's Dracula* (1992) is, in many respects, one of the most faithful adaptations of the novel. But it does introduce a supernatural and romantic link between Dracula and Mina Harker. By making her the apparent reincarnation of his lost love, the woman he sold his soul to revive, Coppola provides a sentimental motive that humanises Dracula as a man driven to extremes by grief.

Mina is a sympathetic character, as is shown in her sensitivity towards Dr Seward and Arthur, and her compassion is even extended to Dracula, but she has only limited existence in her own right. She is aware of her place in society and the home. When she considers her actions, her sense of moral rectitude is absolute and her faith in divine providence is equally firm. Her character most clearly embodies the Christian understanding of suffering, sacrifice and redemption as part of an unknowable divine plan. Her acceptance of her fate as a test of her faith in God and her sentiment 'I am not worthy in His sight' show humility, courage and strength (Chapter 27, pp. 301–2). Her last contribution to the narrative, after her release from Dracula's curse, is not an expression of individual feeling. She describes 'our bitter grief' at the death of Quincey Morris and her last words in the novel record her respect for 'a gallant gentleman' (Chapter 27, p. 314).

LUCY WESTENRA

'Some girls are so vain' (Chapter 5, p. 48). Her own words seem somehow to condemn Lucy. She is completely unaware of the resonances of her remark when she says: 'How true the old proverbs are.' She has the role within the novel of 'the fallen woman', the woman who cannot be saved from herself. Her contrast with Mina is not that of good versus bad, but of sufficient versus insufficient virtue.

Her delight in the attention of the three men is amusing and self-indulgent. The disappointment of the rejected lovers seems to her to be very sad. And her question 'Why can't they let a girl marry three men, or as many as want her' shows her immaturity (Chapter 5, p. 51). Lucy would rather not disappoint any man who flatters her with attention. It also suggests she finds displays of emotion embarrassing and would rather avoid such situations.

Lucy is given some self-deprecating views on her gender which can be seen as partially insightful comments on herself: 'women, I'm afraid, are not always quite as fair as they should be' (Chapter 5, p. 49). Perhaps the most significant is: 'we women are such cowards' (p. 49).

? QUESTION Compare the terms used to describe Lucy and Mina throughout the novel. What differences are there and how are these related to the perspective of the **narrator**?

Lucy has no awareness of the danger she faces even at the moment of her death. She struggles to recall Dracula's attentions – 'something very sweet and very bitter all around me at once' (Chapter 8, p. 82) – and uses the vocabulary of a young child in describing the sensations of her dreams as 'dark and horrid' (Chapter 9, p. 91). Her sense of 'vague fear' is never once defined or taken seriously (p. 91). Her dreams of strange experiences are recalled with laughter and her entire persona seems frivolous and superficial. 'Oceans of love and millions of kisses' she writes to Mina as she delights in her romantic view of the world (Chapter 9, p. 89). At a later stage, as she recovers from a bout of her illness, she is still thinking of her love for Arthur in highly poetic terms: 'health and strength give Love rein' (Chapter 10, p. 106).

For all the wildness and vibrancy in her excitable letters and speech when thinking of her love affairs, Lucy has no real strength of character to call upon in her moment of crisis. Facing death, as she fears she must be, her thoughts are dominated by negatives – 'I dare not' – and she seems helpless (Chapter 11, pp. 119–20). Her request to Van Helsing, 'guard him, and give him peace!', is one of the few moments when her character is not selfish in her outlook (Chapter 12, p. 134). Her transformation to the 'wanton' and 'voluptuous' vampire seems to be the fault of her nature. Dr Seward recalls her former 'pure' beauty as he reacts with horror to the 'unclean' thing she has become (Chapter 16, pp. 175–6). Stoker steadily emphasises the increasing appeal of her physical attraction as Lucy approaches the transformation.

Lucy's strange history embodies the interconnection of sex and death in the Victorian outlook. Her beauty and vanity are warnings to both sexes of the dangers of indulging in the pleasures of the senses. Her 'voluptuousness' is a parody of the Victorian prostitute, a sexually voracious figure that combines the fears of sex, disease and death.

DR ABRAHAM VAN HELSING

Part of Dr Van Helsing's role is to drag the sceptic Dr Seward towards a more open-minded outlook as he outlines the premises

> **? QUESTION**
> Lucy Westenra and Mina Harker are often thought of as the most passive characters in *Dracula*. What active role, if any, do they take within the narrative?

for accepting belief in the supernatural. He only steps into the role of **narrator** on a few occasions, mostly towards the end of the novel. He recounts his adventures in Castle Dracula, the 'butcher work' of dealing with the three vampire ladies, in his own voice (Chapter 27, pp. 308–9). Most of his other activities are reported by Dr Seward, his doubting younger protégé.

Van Helsing is the acceptable face of the foreigner in the novel. His language and his religion set him apart from the other characters, but his reputation and store of wisdom (old and new) recommend him. He is under personal obligation to his middle-class English pupil, whose trust alone is enough to grant him entry to this society. His name is sometimes associated with an aristocratic background, but unlike the Germanic 'von', which implies an inherited social status, 'van' in Dutch usually means 'from' and locates a family to a place or region. Helsing, despite its ominous and diabolical sound, is related more generally to Scandinavian words for 'narrow waterway'. This may be interpreted as an implication that this character is on the 'strait and narrow' path, a righteous character.

Van Helsing appears in the second phase of the novel and is brought in to rescue Lucy. In this task he is outwitted by his opponent, and the rest of the novel is a battle of wits and wills between him and Count Dracula. His personal characteristics are similar to those of the Count. His temperament is explained in brief indicators; Dr Seward apologises for his old teacher's 'arbitrary' manner (Chapter 9, p. 94). Mina notes the facial features that indicate a dominant personality and mentions also his 'reddish' hair. Though this is never explicitly stated, the notion that there is something fierce about his temper is clearly suggested.

Van Helsing appears to be adept at presenting himself to other characters in ways that suit his purpose. He is charming and frivolous with Lucy when examining her; serious and warm when greeting Mina as a married woman. He has a sense of humour and compassion: 'King Laugh' is something he understands well (Chapter 13, pp. 145–6). Mina gives the most detailed view of Van Helsing. Her clear impression is of a man of 'thought and power'.

? QUESTION
Dracula has no reflection, but Van Helsing is his mirror image. What is the effect of this unity of opposites in the novel?

CHECK THE FILM
The 2004 film *Van Helsing*, directed by Stephen Sommers, depicted a very different Van Helsing to the one created by Stoker. The role of the vampire slayer was played by an actor in his mid thirties, Hugh Jackman, and his Van Helsing was an action hero whose enemies included not just Count Dracula but also Frankenstein's monster, a werewolf and Mr Hyde.

CHECK THE NET

Charles Darwin's *Expression of the Emotions in Man and Animals* (1873) detailed observations that contribute to the notion of predetermined characteristics and personality types. You can read this text, and others by Darwin, at www.darwin-literature.com

CONTEXT

Earlier Gothic tales, written from a Protestant viewpoint, used the **genre** to criticise the Roman Catholic Church for promoting superstition. In *Dracula*, Stoker seems to be both returning to and inverting the externalised terrors of the early Gothic tale. Stoker dwells on the horror of doubtful certainty as a psychological dilemma but places the source of internal or psychic stress clearly in the physical world.

The adjectives she attaches to his features convey his character: 'noble', 'resolute', 'sensitive', 'tender or stern' (Chapter 14, p. 151).

Van Helsing is the character who is able to bring in 'the weapons of superstition', as Stoker described the **symbols** of the Roman Catholic Church. There is no problem for him, as a metaphysician and scholar, in dealing with esoteric mysteries on an equal scientific basis with more mundane and explicable phenomena. This is the open-mindedness that Dr Seward admires but finds difficult to adopt as his own belief. Van Helsing is a champion of truth but accommodates knowledge of all kinds into his world view. As he says, a 'small truth' may be valuable, but it is not 'all the truth in the universe' (Chapter 14, p. 160).

It is suggested, in a very obscure manner, that Van Helsing may have lost his son to a vampire. He speaks at Lucy's funeral of Arthur reminding him of his son. Near the end, as he destroys the vampire women, he speaks of his 'motive for hate' as something exceptional (Chapter 27, p. 308). This may be a rather speculative reading. In any case, the fact that the great Van Helsing is nearly distracted from his purpose by the 'mere presence' of the women shows his own limitations and the strength of the enemy. As paralysis threatens, Van Helsing is saved by Mina's scream. He too has to be rescued by the love of a good woman from the temptations of the 'voluptuous' demons.

Throughout the latter half of the novel, Van Helsing is the leader of the fight to save Lucy and Mina. He persuades and organises the men. His medical skill is insufficient to keep Lucy or Renfield alive, but it is his knowledge of faith that saves Mina. He combines the roles of priest and scientist, though it is obvious he is more religious and more Catholic in his outlook than any other character. He is given the last speech in the novel, a defiant repudiation of his own methods of investigation up to this point: 'We want no proofs; we ask none to believe us!' (Note, p. 315). This is the exact opposite of a scientific outlook. Van Helsing's reassurance that the son will learn to appreciate his mother's goodness is an elitist view of the world. Other people's views are of no importance.

By the end of the novel Van Helsing has travelled further in his beliefs than might at first glance be appreciated. His first counsel to Dr Seward was 'knowledge is stronger than memory, and we should not trust the weaker'. He also pointed out: 'We learn from failure, not from success!' (Chapter 10, p. 100). It could be said that he has learnt much over the course of his development, as they repeatedly fail to protect the women from Dracula. This also explains the need for Quincey's sacrifice. Without this failure, what would be the lesson of defeating Dracula? This is why Van Helsing draws attention to the daring love of the men and why the lesson is embodied in the child that bears the American's name.

Arthur Holmwood, Lord Godalming

This scion of a noble English family is the third man to be introduced by Lucy and, in his social rank, name and title, represents the heritage of the English aristocracy. His first name, Arthur, draws upon legends of chivalry, magic and kingship, and can be interpreted as 'bear man' or 'Thor's man'. Either meaning gives the impression of great strength or solidity. Holmwood, in its meanings of 'oak grove' or 'wooded island', could be a reference to Britain as an island nation; Godalming is a reference to the Saxon ancestry. Both surnames also relate to places in the county of Surrey, one of the Home Counties, typically and definitively 'English'. While these kind of values are often now thought of as middle-class, it would be ridiculous to see this character as anything other than a representative of the feudal tradition that created the English aristocracy. His bearing and manner are the **antithesis** of the cruel despotism of the other aristocrat in the novel. He is a benevolent member of the ruling class, who takes advantage of his social position only when circumstances oblige him to act for the greater good.

Arthur is in the background for a while before stepping forward to play his part in dutifully dispatching the doomed Lucy. He calls in Dr Seward to care for Lucy when she appears to be suffering from 'no special disease' (Chapter 9, p. 92). His duties, as son and heir, oblige him to be with his dying father during the crisis of Lucy's illness. He is momentarily able to attend in time to be the first to make the blood sacrifice on her behalf, but then the 'brave lover' is sent away in

CHECK THE BOOK
David Rogers suggests in his introduction to the 2000 Wordsworth Classics edition of *Dracula* that Stoker invites us to read Lord Godalming's name as 'Lord God Almighty or even Lord Gold Aiming, the aim of his affection being the blonde, "pure" Lucy' (p. xv).

ignorance of the real threat to his fiancée (Chapter 10, p. 103). When he returns, though her condition is much worse, he displays the fortitude of his class as he comforts her through the death scene. His 'stalwart manhood' is severely tested by the emotional strain (Chapter 13, p. 139). His grief is expressed to Dr Seward: 'there is nothing left in the wide world for me to live for' (p. 140).

Though amazed and outraged by the plan to visit Lucy's tomb, Arthur goes along with Van Helsing because he has pledged his trust. He is, above all else, an honourable man who will do what is right, regardless of the consequences. He voices true shock at the perversion of his beloved Lucy to a parasitic monster: 'There can be no horror like this ever any more!' (Chapter 16, p. 176). As he drives his stake into Lucy's heart with a hammer, he becomes himself again, 'like a figure of Thor' (p. 179). In this mercy killing Arthur reclaims or achieves his true manhood. The **symbolic** sexual representations of masculinity are also significant in this moment of reclamation. The hammer, representing strength, and the stake, a phallic symbol of virility, are emblems of male potency used to reclaim not only Arthur's challenged manhood but Lucy's womanhood stolen by a deceitful foreign aristocrat. Arthur is clearly positioned as the noble defender of his family's (and his country's) bloodline.

Arthur, afterwards, is able to 'break down' and release his grief in front of Mina without it being 'derogatory to his manhood' (Chapter 17, p. 191). Quincey Morris shows 'delicacy' in withdrawing to allow Mina to play mother to Arthur's 'wearied child' as his tears and sobs flow without restraint. He does not share Dr Seward's capacity for doubt. Fortified by the comforting sympathy of a good woman, Arthur contributes wholeheartedly to the work of tracking down and destroying Dracula. Using his title, his wealth and his amateur skills in sailing and engineering, he is fully committed to the campaign. His firmness of purpose is rewarded with a happy marriage.

QUINCEY P. MORRIS

Described as 'such a nice fellow, an American from Texas', this character is 'really well educated and has exquisite manners', who

CONTEXT

The vernacular expressions of the young American nation seemed to have an immediate appeal for young Victorians, while the older generation frowned upon slang as barbaric speech. Similar attitudes to standard American English still exist.

only talks 'American slang' to amuse Lucy Westenra (Chapter 5, pp. 49–50). Through him we learn of the adventurous past of the main trio of the band that will form to hunt Dracula. Their friendship survives their rivalry in love. Although he may be of the New World, Quincey has Old World values of honour and gallantry. Again, his name is a clue here. It is a family name that has branches in Wales, Scotland and Ireland. So perhaps Quincey represents in some way a gathering of the clans or a return to the roots of his country's origin.

Quincey's role in the novel is to complete the fellowship that resists the invader and to assist heroically in the destruction of the enemy. This may be **symbolic** of the so-called 'special relationship' supposed to exist between Britain and the United States of America. At the time, Britain and the other older European empires were beginning to realise that America was the new rising imperial power, so there is perhaps an idealised wish embodied in this character that the English-speaking world should be united in the face of the foreign competition. Quincey affirms his friendship and respect for Lucy and Mina; he shows sympathetic support for his friend Arthur in his grief; and he willingly trusts Dr Seward and Van Helsing. He is a powerful ally.

Quincey is identified as a man of action and modern weaponry. He is keen to make use of the most advanced military technology available in the form of the Winchester repeating rifle. He shoots first and asks questions later, though he is the first to ask the rather obvious question about what removed so much blood from Lucy. He is the first to speak after Van Helsing asks for the men's permission to visit Lucy's tomb and open her coffin, even though he admits he doesn't 'quite see his drift': 'but I swear he's honest, and that's good enough for me' (Chapter 15, p. 170); and when Mina asks them to promise to kill her if she is 'so changed that it is better that I die that I may live', he is 'the first to rise after the pause' and swear that he will 'not flinch from the duty' (Chapter 25, pp. 275–6).

It is Quincey's readiness to leap into the battle with older weapons that costs him his life. He is struck down by a gypsy loyal to Dracula and dies a noble death. However, he is rewarded with the sight of the curse lifted from Mina's forehead. He dies, 'with a

CONTEXT

Texas became the twenty-eighth state in the United States of America in 1845. It was part of the Confederacy that lost the Civil War (1861–5) and was only readmitted to the Union in 1870. Renfield's appraisal of the state's significant role in the rising dominance of the American empire (Chapter 18, p. 203) is curiously prophetic: Texas's oil reserves were discovered four years later in 1901.

CONTEXT

Bram Stoker admired American authors and had met some of his literary heroes when visiting America with Henry Irving's theatre company.

QUESTION
The character Renfield is often presented in film versions of Dracula as merely a madman with repulsive eating habits or a simple slave of his 'Master'. To what extent is this true to Stoker's development of Renfield's character and his role within the narrative?

CHECK THE FILM
Christopher Lee reprised his role as Count Dracula in the 1966 *Dracula: Prince of Darkness*, directed by Terence Fisher. The character of Ludwig, an insect-eating lunatic, is clearly based on Stoker's Renfield.

CONTEXT
Vlad Tepes – also known as Vlad the Impaler on account of his fondness for impaling enemies on spikes – was a fifteenth-century Balkan ruler. A cruel and ruthless warrior, he was also well educated and a successful politician.

smile', as 'a gallant gentleman', and his name lives on in the next generation of the Harker family.

R. M. RENFIELD

Dr Seward's initial interest in Renfield is aroused because he is 'so unlike the normal lunatic' (Chapter 5, p. 52). Dr Seward envies the madman's sense of purpose, despite its grotesque manifestation in a diet of live insects. As a character, there is very little to Renfield's development. He has two or three levels of activity: frenetic mania, violent frenzy and curiously charming lucidity. By his own account he is 'as sane as at least the majority of men who are in full possession of their liberties' (Chapter 18, p. 203). There is an immediate connection with Dracula that is not explained. Beyond the coincidence of his interest in defeating death through consuming life (an obvious reference to legends of cannibalism) there is no reason given for Renfield adopting Dracula as his 'Master'.

His main function is to act as an indicator of the Count's presence in and around Carfax and the asylum. He is the one who grants Dracula access to the asylum, endangering Mina. Renfield's late resistance to the Count seems selfishly motivated, but could also be interpreted as a deathbed conversion inspired by a wish to protect Mina. His bloody and painful death is a fitting punishment for his treachery. Renfield represents another model of human arrogance in pursuit of knowledge and he too pays the price for assuming he might become immortal, recalling the old wisdom of the Greek dramatist Euripides: 'Those whom God wishes to destroy, he first makes mad.'

COUNT DRACULA

Stoker's vampire is a point of departure from vampires in legend or literature. He tells Jonathan Harker: 'Our ways are not your ways, and there shall be to you many strange things' (Chapter 2, p. 19). He is more closely rooted in suggested historical reference and given a more rounded story of origin than any other vampire. Whether or not Stoker based his character on an actual historical figure, the apparent coincidences that link Count Dracula to real tyrannical rulers have created an appeal for some readers who like to blur the edges of fantasy and reality.

Count Dracula casts no reflection. He can change shape and assume the form of many different animals, even appearing as a mist. His insubstantial shapelessness allows many fears to be reflected in the reading of his character. Stoker has Jonathan Harker read Dracula's personality from his features in the second chapter. His class, his personal characteristics and his nature single him out as a selfish, egotistical creature. He is a parasite and a contagion. He is a man but he is animalistic. He is not mortal but nor is he immortal or invulnerable. He has irresistible powers of hypnotic mind control; he can enslave people against their will to do his bidding.

Dracula represents a foreign threat to the British or Western way of life. He is a 'noble' but is a debased and cruel aristocrat. His superficial, deceitful charm is contrasted with the manners of the true English aristocracy in Arthur, Lord Godalming. There is also a suggestion that Dracula has exhausted his position in Transylvania; the vampire dynasty is unable to grow without invading new territories. Is Dracula ready to become more powerful or is he on the run from a population that has seen him for what he is and begun to protect itself? The connections here to the nineteenth century in Europe as a revolutionary and unsettled historical period can be interpreted in many ways.

The Count is, most of all, seen in Castle Dracula in the first phase of the novel. His manipulation of Jonathan Harker preserves his mystery while providing a very disturbing hint of his menace. His need for power is summed up in the very simple phrase 'none other should be master of me' (Chapter 2, p. 19). Throughout the second phase of the novel, his presence is glimpsed in evidence given by **narrators** entirely unaware of the danger. Dracula never disappears from the narrative entirely but is not seen for the bulk of the novel and is more often discussed than described. He appears as himself again in two scenes in the third phase. He forces Mina to drink his blood and he escapes the ambush set by the men. In these moments of direct appearance Dracula displays the same cruel delight in playing with his enemies as he did when tormenting Jonathan in his captivity. We are given a glimpse of his own sense of historical enormity, of himself as person 'who commanded nations, and intrigued for them, and fought for them, hundreds of years before they were born' (Chapter 21, p. 239). His taunt to the men is loaded

CONTEXT

Phrenology dates from the late eighteenth century and is associated with the Viennese physician Dr Franz Gall (1758–1828), who believed that there was a relationship between facial features and character, specifically between the shape of the head and the intellect.

 CHECK THE NET

The common assumption that Stoker's Count Dracula is based on the historical despot Vlad Tepes is a matter of academic dispute. Find Dr Elizabeth Miller's website, Dracula's Homepage, at **www.mun.ca** by searching for 'Dracula'.

CHECK THE BOOK

Dracula: Prince of Many Faces by Radu R. Florescu and Raymond T. McNally (1989) is an informative biography of the fifteenth-century prince of Romania, Vlad Dracula. In it the authors describe his life and career, and examine the comparisons between the real-life Dracula and Stoker's fictional Count.

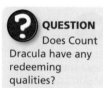

QUESTION

Does Count Dracula have any redeeming qualities?

CHECK THE BOOK

'Better to reign in hell, than serve in heaven' (John Milton, *Paradise Lost*, Book I, line 263). Milton's Lucifer seems to provide a model for Dracula and his sentiment 'I would be master still' (Chapter 2, p. 19). The biblical figures of the fallen angel, the fallen man and the fallen woman are intertwined in Stoker's novel.

with contempt and sexual ambiguity: 'Your girls that you all love are mine already' (Chapter 23, p. 255).

Dracula possesses people only as a means of controlling others. He has no interest in individuals beyond what they offer him, either as a source of food or furtherance of his interests. He tells the vampire women in Chapter 3: 'Yes, I too can love; you yourselves can tell it from the past' (p. 34). But this is the only evidence given of his capacity for love. The sexual power he exudes is more to do with dominance, ruthlessness and command. Arrogance, for some, is a particularly appealing characteristic with great erotic potential. To be the slave of a powerful master is certainly Renfield's wish, which suggests **ambivalence**, at least, in the sexual orientation of the relationship.

The last sight of the Count is as he wakes, mistakenly thinking he has triumphed and a fraction too late to defend himself in the final battle. The 'look of peace' on his face at the moment of his destruction, a delightful surprise to Mina Harker, signifies his release from an unhappy existence (Chapter 27, p. 314). It also creates a slight softening of Dracula's monstrosity, and this gives Mina a chance to display true Christian forgiveness towards her enemy and demonstrate the healing power of pity. It recalls that he was once a human being and, as it is only in death that anyone truly finds peace, the change of expression shows Dracula has been humanised by death. In this way, he can be seen as a quasi-tragic figure expressing man's folly of ambition and arrogance. This might have greater impact, perhaps, if the novel as a whole were not so **melodramatic**. Dracula is the villain of the piece, to be booed off stage and resoundingly defeated by the heroes of the hour.

THEMES

RELIGION AND THE SUPERNATURAL

Bram Stoker tells a tale that resolves into a Manichaean conflict between the forces of good and the forces of evil. Earth is merely a battleground for these metaphysical entities to contest the ownership of the soul of humanity. Dracula is a powerful demon, a willing servant of the devil and a manifestation of pure evil. Van Helsing is an angel of mercy and an avenging servant of the Lord. Both characters are serving higher powers in acting out their plans.

Gothic tales typically make use of supernatural beings and forces that require superstitious belief in extraordinary realms beyond the norms of nature and beyond the limits of accepted beliefs. A rationally minded atheist might see little difference between superstition and faith, but the distinction is crucial to a person of religious outlook. Stoker introduces the notion of extraordinary phenomena early in the first phase of the novel. The 'blue flames' seen by Jonathan Harker and explained by Count Dracula are the most obvious example of something above and beyond the norms of nature. The 'uncanny' relationship between the Count and the wolves – his 'children of the night', wild and dangerous in nature but tamed by his very thoughts – develops throughout the novel. Dracula's mutability of corporeal substance and his lack of reflection or shadow place him well outside the accepted laws of physical nature. There can be no such thing; yet there he remains, stubbornly existing in defiance of all rational explanation (see **Literary background: The Gothic tradition** and **The vampire in literature**).

Atmospheric ruins that inspire nervous thoughts of 'spooks' and ghosts also feature in Gothic tales. The skeletal ruins of Whitby Abbey that Stoker incorporates in *Dracula* are a relic of the thirteenth century. Not only does the site have its own legends of hauntings and miraculous saints, it combines religion and the supernatural in its own ruined, ancient form. There is a suggestion of violence in the broken walls and windows. The eerie, dismembered architecture of this abandoned and desolate place of worship overlooks the mood of the narrative in its second main phase.

The debate about the supernatural, and how possible it is to believe in the impossible, is mostly carried on by the characters on the side of good. After all, a demon has no need to doubt its own existence or suffer much existential angst about its purpose. The only wicked character to show any concern for the soul is Renfield, who seems disturbed when Dr Seward questions him on the subject. The distinction between a demon and a madman, traditionally seen as 'possessed by demons', is enough to explain his quibbling dismissal

> **CONTEXT**
>
> Manichaeism was a dualistic religion with Christian, Gnostic and pagan elements. Founded in Persia in the third century by Manichaeus or Mani, known as the Apostle of Light (c.215–c.276), the religion was based on a primeval conflict between light and darkness.

RELIGION AND THE SUPERNATURAL continued

CONTEXT
On 24 May 1897 Stoker wrote a letter to William Gladstone in which he said: 'It is a story of a vampire – the old mediaeval vampire but recrudescent today … The book is necessarily full of horrors and terrors but I trust that these are calculated to "cleanse the mind by pity & terror".' Stoker's use of this phrase has important links with the idea of catharsis. This is the cleansing process by which a literary text, especially a tragic or dramatic one, draws out heightened emotions from the audience with the objective of purifying them. Its origins are in Greek drama and the writings of the philosopher Aristotle.

of the souls whose lives he consumes. Dracula is interested in making everyone his 'creatures', and the vampire women are interested only in 'kisses'.

Viewed in this light, the novel becomes more than a romantic adventure with a highly moral 'lesson' about the dangers of sexuality (based on a defined set of gender expectations). It is a kind of lengthy **exposition** of the necessity of religious faith that appeals unashamedly to superstition in its argument. It makes use of horror, a kind of primitive aversion therapy, with the purpose of instructing the reader in the consequences of certain personal choices. That Stoker would submit such a book to William Gladstone, the former prime minister, for his approval is not so surprising. Gladstone had taken an interest in the issue of prostitution, in 1848 founding the Church Penitentiary Association for the Reclamation of Fallen Women; he was closely involved in the political questions of Ireland, and in retirement was pursuing his literary interests.

Stoker, with his Protestant family background and upbringing in Ireland, would have been only too aware of the sectarian significance of his story. There is a deliberate anomaly in the use of the **symbols** of the Roman Catholic faith that would have been easily shocking to the readership of his time. The issues of doctrine and symbols are at the heart of the differences between these two faiths. The way the nominally Anglican characters are enabled to adopt the characteristics of the Roman Catholic faith can be read in various ways. Is it an ecumenical position arguing for greater cooperation between forms of Christianity? Is it an abandonment of the more strictly rationalised faith of the Anglican Church? Is it an identification of Roman Catholicism with superstition? The underlying message may be that the horrors and evils in the world need a more aggressive response than the more traditionally tolerant Anglican view.

Is the novel any more than a superficial or decorative expansion on the **themes** of redemption and loss? The theatricality of the 'weapons of superstition' (a phrase used by Stoker in his letter to Gladstone) and their effectiveness is one of the most vivid images of the story. Dr Seward, the sceptic, feels the 'mighty power' that makes Dracula cower away from the crucifix (Chapter 23, p. 255).

The novel's assumption of an afterlife is its premise and its chief dynamic. If the soul exists, as is also assumed in the novel, and does survive death then its destination is a matter of some interest. Eternity is a long time to be in the wrong place. The characters in the novel that represent the forces of goodness have a moral obligation, as good Christian folk, to save lost souls.

SCIENCE AND MODERNITY

Dr Seward reflects the confidence of the modern age when he finds it difficult to believe in vampirism and cannot accept 'that such a thing is here in London in the nineteenth century' (Chapter 14, p. 159). He is very much a man of his moment, who desires to make a contribution to the advancement of science. It is his cause, but he is unable to realise this ambition.

The nineteenth century was a time of almost unprecedented technological and scientific advancement. Alongside theories that have retained scientific credibility were many other views competing for attention, as interest in phenomena and the possibilities of science increased rapidly. These are now referred to as 'pseudoscience' and Van Helsing lists a number of the theories discredited by the late nineteenth century in his discussion with Dr Seward. Dr Seward sums up his own dilemma: 'I do not know what to think, and I have no data on which to found a conjecture' (Chapter 14, p. 158).

The objects that characters use define their relationship to the modern world. Dr Seward and Lucy Westenra have a phonograph, but only he uses it to record his diary. Mina and Jonathan Harker are trained in the art of stenography or shorthand writing, and Mina travels with a portable typewriter. Arthur Holmwood plays with steamboats; Quincey Morris likes the Winchester repeating rifle. Van Helsing makes a rare venture into the modern world when he uses a phonograph, but is mostly associated with books and religious **symbols**.

The nineteenth century was the age of steam and the age of railway expansion, with thousands of miles of track being laid to connect parts of the world more speedily than before. The 'men of the

---

CONTEXT

At the beginning of the nineteenth century there were no railway tracks in Britain. By 1860 there were over ten thousand miles of tracks laid, and passenger traffic was an established part of the trade. Great speculative profits were made in the construction and financing of the railways. Numerous accidents did eventually lead to legislation for safety standards, but competition did very little to ensure these standards. By the end of the century there were thirty-five thousand miles of track and nine thousand new railway stations.

world', aided by their 'pearl among women', use the railway to outflank Dracula, who travels by less advanced methods – a sailing ship and horse-drawn wagon.

Van Helsing and Dr Seward are the chief participants in the debate on scientific method. The scientists are brought into conflict with the supernatural, and their rational view of the world is broadened to accommodate the irrational and inexplicable. The characters who take modern technology as a kind of fetish, a mundane expression of their faith in scientific progress, learn to value and respect religious objects. The philosophical conflict initiated by Charles Darwin's *On the Origin of Species by Means of Natural Selection* in 1859 is not specifically referred to in this debate. In the novel, as in much of the public controversy over Darwinism, it is not the real implications of the theory of evolution that are debated. There is no question mark over the nature of creation and the existence or otherwise of God for Dr Seward. The compatibility of religion with a scientific view of the world is not a concern for these characters. They are far too busy finding a way to incorporate superstition 'scientifically' into their religion.

LAW AND CIVILISATION

Jonathan Harker is a solicitor, only one of the solicitors that have dealings with Dracula. Dracula makes use of the agents of the legal profession to potentially subvert the institutions of law and order in the civilised world. The Count is an arbiter of life and death in his own country. He can set his wolves on inconvenient protesters to silence them. He steals children with impunity and appropriates the wealth of the dead as he sees fit.

Van Helsing has a legal as well as a medical background, but he operates within and beyond the strict boundaries of the law of the land. Dr Seward and he can cover up the inconvenient deaths to prevent intrusive investigation by other authorities. He advises a peer of the realm on the best means of fraudulently gaining access to Dracula's house. These abuses are excused in the story by their higher motivation, as Van Helsing has the defence that he is following a higher law.

CHECK THE BOOK

American writer Anne Rice (1941–) is the author of the Vampire Chronicles, a series of novels revolving around the character Lestat de Lioncourt, a French nobleman turned into a vampire in the eighteenth century. Rice's vampires are different in many ways to Stoker's Dracula: they are not shape-shifters; they are unaffected by crucifixes or garlic; and they cannot be killed with a wooden stake. The first in the series, *Interview with the Vampire* (1976), was made into a film starring Tom Cruise and Brad Pitt in 1994.

It is a curious feature of the story that Dracula is able to establish a base of operations in England legally and the men cannot avoid breaking the law in their bid to expel him from the country. Dracula's bases are established around London, but Piccadilly is a prime spot, exactly at the heart of the capital of the British Empire. The suggestion is that there is a corruption at the core of civilisation and the crisis threatens to overwhelm even the wealthiest and most powerful. The skirmish with Dracula at this location is a highly significant victory for the men, despite Dracula's escape.

The qualities of Western civilisation are represented most of all in the people of Stoker's story. Apart from the nobility, the middle-class professions and the ex-colonial allies, the working-class characters represent a kind of healthy cheekiness and yeoman-like stoicism in the face of the foreign threat. They all know their place and carry out their allotted duties in the way that England expects. The sense of national pride, and pride in the British Empire, is present in all the English characters, but it is expressed in terms of praise for their personal qualities rather than national characteristics. As Mina says, 'Oh, thank God for good brave men!' (Chapter 23, p. 259). Dracula, in his identity as foreigner, and an ambassador of evil, is very clearly represented as 'other' to all that is just and good.

THE NEW WOMAN

The notion of the 'New Woman' was in part a reaction to the increasing moves towards emancipation and economic independence for women. Middle-class women who had ambitions beyond marriage, domesticity and child-rearing were ridiculed and portrayed as either promiscuous or deluded. Much of the discussion was created by, and limited to, the press.

Neither Lucy nor Mina thinks of herself as a 'New Woman', and they respond to the most 'exciting' or 'shocking' aspects of the notion with some amusement. Stoker gives the two women different elements of the caricatured female: Lucy is flirtatious, indulgent and romantic; Mina is diligent and organised. Stoker's reaction to the new femininity is to kill off the foolish virgin and marry off the wise one.

> **CONTEXT**
>
> *A Vindication of the Rights of Woman* by Mary Wollstonecraft (1792) was part of the political discussion responding to the French Revolution. Written in response to Thomas Paine's *The Rights of Man* (1791), it called for equal rights and opportunities for women in the new era of progress. The fuss in the late nineteenth-century press about the 'New Woman' shows how little attitudes had changed.

MADNESS

'Sleep has no place it can call its own' (Chapter 23, p. 260) says Mina Harker when questioned under hypnosis. The exploration of madness and dreaming is a **conventional** feature of the Gothic **genre**. Many of Stoker's characters have difficulty sleeping and question their own sanity. The treatment of mental disorder and the developing notion of mental health care were nineteenth-century advances in medicine. Private asylums such as Dr Seward's establishment were starting to make a difference to the earlier 'Bedlam' arrangements where patients were often treated as a spectacle for entertainment. Medical science was also beginning to investigate the realms of the unconscious. Psychology, as a distinct study, was beginning to form an identity under the leadership of Sigmund Freud.

Lucy has a history of disturbed sleep. Mina's dreams, like Lucy's, are evidence of Dracula's hypnotic interference. Dr Seward is prevented from sleeping by his thoughts of Lucy and administers his own chemical cure. Jonathan Harker hopes his reality is a dream but finds it is dangerous to sleep outside his own bedroom. Van Helsing and others go without sleep in the vain hope of affecting the course of events. Restful sleep occasionally restores a character to health or to a sane perspective, but only for the nightmares to return.

The 'Un-Dead' are said to be sleeping in their tombs. Lucy, as a beautiful corpse, looks more alive and appears to be sleeping. Seances, where spirit mediums make use of a trance or sleep to contact the spirits of the departed, were a familiar part of the popular craze for spiritualism. The **metaphorical** link between sleep, death and the supposed eternal afterlife comes into Stoker's use of the vulnerability of the sleeper. At the heart of this is the rationalisation of the fear that, if we sleep, one day we might not wake up.

CONTEXT

Bedlam was a corruption of Bethlehem in the name of the Hospital of St Mary of Bethlehem, a priory founded in 1247 in London. It began to receive lunatics in the late fourteenth century, and became a hospital for lunatics in 1547. By the seventeenth century it was one of the sights of London, where for a few pence anyone could view the inmates and bait them.

CHECK THE BOOK

The Interpretation of Dreams was published by Sigmund Freud (1856–1939) in 1899. In it he discusses the importance of analysing dreams in accessing and understanding the unconscious.

NARRATIVE TECHNIQUES

THE EPISTOLARY NOVEL

Stoker's fragmentary, quasi-historical grouping of documents creates the multiple narrative perspectives in *Dracula*. It is an elaborate development of the literary form known as the epistolary novel. There are many novels in which the narrative is created in a series of letters between characters. The form was well known in the eighteenth century but was considered quite unusual or even old-fashioned by the end of the nineteenth century. In 1860 Wilkie Collins had made successful use of the epistolary form in *The Woman in White*, considered to be an influence on Stoker in the writing of *Dracula*.

The technique positions the reader to identify with each of the **narrators** in turn, experiencing the events and their feelings from shifting and often contradictory points of view. This disrupts the tendency for the reader to identify with or give privileged credibility to any one narrator. It also creates a distance between the author and the reader, mediating the text through another layer of meaning.

Stoker incorporates the notion of writing as an unreliable record of experience into his epistolary form. This question mark over the authenticity of the text is established in the prefatory note and is an important signifier of Stoker's key philosophical motif of the uncertainty of existence. But he makes his characters aware that their faith in an accurate historical record and its power to convince the reader of the literal truth of the tale are not necessarily the same thing at all. Stoker's borrowed paradox of faith, as 'that which enables us to believe things which we know to be untrue' (Chapter 14, p. 160), could quite easily be applied to the creative act of narrative reading per se. We each read *Dracula* with our own understanding of 'nature's eccentricities and possible impossibilities' (to quote Dr Seward, p. 160).

The author has his characters construct the narrative not only from personal letters but from a wide range of written and spoken language. There are journal entries that are transcriptions of shorthand notes or wax-cylinder phonographic recordings,

CHECK THE BOOK

Earlier examples of the epistolary novel are Samuel Richardson's *Pamela* (1740) and *Clarissa* (1748).

handwritten memoranda, telegrams, business letters from solicitors, newspaper reports which give second- or third-hand accounts of events, and unreliable verbal translations from foreign languages. The narrative often proceeds without a defining voice and developments are often communicated by individuals who lack any existence beyond their functional relevance to the plot. There are many **expositions** of plot detail by minor characters with no personal relationship to the main characters. The linguistic range of the narrative includes formal and informal **tone**, standard English, dialect, archaic expression, personal memoir, reportage and much else. Stoker delineates his characters through the form of their language as well as the content of their opinions or personality.

TIME AND PLACE

Major developments in the plot are defined and contained by location, rather than by chronological sequence. There are times in the narrative where the presentation of events is affected by the order of reports shifting backwards and forwards. Some reports predict events and others report after the fact. Seemingly innocuous and unrelated reports are suffused with greater significance by their position within the narrative sequence. In *Dracula* the unsettled linearity of the multiple narratives disrupts the orderly, civilised telling of the tale attempted by each of the **narrators**.

Castle Dracula frames the novel at the start and climax. Stoker's endnote is not given a location and wanders between England and Transylvania as a kind of summary of the novel. The keynote location is the 'wild and uncanny' mountain stronghold in all its 'grandeur' (as Mina describes it in Chapter 27). It is a fortress and a prison.

The second phase of the novel continues the Gothic architectural **theme** in the romantic ruins of the abbey at Whitby, Yorkshire. The graveyard is central to the action and the mood of this locale is almost claustrophobic in its doom-laden intensity. Carfax in Purfleet, Essex, takes the reader again to another ruin of a house. Alongside these ruins Dr Seward's asylum, the Westenra home at Hillingham, Dracula's house in Piccadilly, London, and the Harkers' home in Exeter, Devon, are spaces unworthy of description. The third phase of the novel returns often to the grounds and chapel of Carfax.

> **CONTEXT**
>
> Transylvania has become a popular setting for horror stories, particularly vampire tales, since the publication of *Dracula*.

It is the outline of the 'broken battlements' of Castle Dracula that dominates the imaginary horizon of the narrative (Chapter 1, p. 13; Chapter 2, p. 22; and Chapter 27, p. 314). Appropriately set against the 'moonlit sky' at the start and against the 'light of the setting sun' at the end, the castle is left standing in our thoughts by Jonathan Harker's return visit when he sees it 'reared high above a waste of desolation' (Note, p. 315). This is a stark warning that evil is never fully defeated and is a tempting invitation to a sequel that many who came after Stoker could not resist.

STRUCTURE

The novel can be divided into four sections or phases (or, indeed, movements or acts – the latter term would be completely appropriate for this camp theatrical romp). The first phase deals with Dracula's preparation of the invasion of England and the imprisonment of Jonathan Harker. The second phase is clearly divided from the first as the focus shifts from Transylvania to England. The action of the second phase is Dracula's invasion of England and the seduction of Lucy. The assault on the civilised world continues into the third phase, which truly gets going when the men gather together to begin the defence of the realm. The fourth phase of the novel is the shortest and is concerned with the pursuit of Dracula back to his home country for vengeance and the salvation of the good women of Britain.

LANGUAGE

Stoker's narrative language is dominated by the forms he chooses for the perspective of the narrators. Some of the texts function within the narrative without obviously providing a narrator as such; the writers who produce these 'documents' are informants rather than participants. As such, the structure leads to a style which ebbs and flows, with strange contrasts and sudden excitements punctuating the slower, meandering currents of the plot. Much of the writing is taken up with the relating of events by participants or observers and there are very few passages of descriptive writing.

CONTEXT

The word 'vampire' comes via the French from the Hungarian *vampir*, which is possibly related to the Turkish *uber*, meaning 'witch', and the Russian word for vampire, *upyr*.

Though much of the narrative is in the mode of telling rather than showing, it is also true that Stoker's **narrators** show us a great deal in their telling. The success of Stoker's use of **irony** depends on the audience understanding the parts of the story that each narrator cannot tell.

? QUESTION
What is the effect of the various forms of language used to depict the working-class characters' dialogue and the speech of the major characters?

Most of the novel's narrators share a belief in the power of language, particularly written language, to represent reality and reveal truth. For them, the act of writing is a sacred duty and ritual for understanding the world around them. Stoker plays with a variety of forms of writing: personal journals and diaries kept in shorthand or transcribed from sound recordings; personal letters; business letters; telegrams; newspaper journalism; medical reports; nautical records; memoranda and notes of various purposes.

In Chapter 11 Stoker moves from the contented childishness of Lucy's diary – 'Good-night everybody' – to the terse professionalism of Dr Seward's casebook: 'Let all be put down exactly' (p. 111). The chronological inversion of the narrative at this point is accompanied by the amused tones of the educated professional reporter 'perpetually using the words *Pall Mall Gazette* as a sort of talisman' when dealing with his social inferiors (p. 113). The reporter's laconic humour about sharing a room with a wolf is detached and self-deprecating: 'I have always thought that a wild animal never looks so well as when some obstacle of pronounced durability is between us; a personal experience has intensified rather than diminished that idea' (p. 117). The fictional writer is clearly shaping an epigram for the amusement of an equally fictional reader, but the use of comic relief here is a deliberate structural ploy on Stoker's part. A rapid succession of events is communicated over two short extracts from Dr Seward connected by a telegram from Van Helsing. Dr Seward, weary after being attacked by Renfield – 'I need rest, rest, rest' (p. 118) – is galvanised by the abrupt imperative of his mentor's delayed telegram: 'Do not fail'. Dr Seward's next sentence has the interrupted syntax of a telegram, 'Just off for train to London', immediately conveying the urgency of his response. The **tone** of Lucy's memorandum is pathetic, as she is too weak to write (and a weak writer) but knows that writing 'must be done if I die in the doing' (p. 118).

Stoker's language is deftly delineated to the voice of each narrator. Reported speech becomes the defining feature of the main characters. Much of the novel is in an informal and personal style appropriate to an intimate record of personal reminiscence.

Understatement and hyperbole are the most obvious contrasting forms of language in *Dracula*: Stoker undercuts the horror of some incidents and emphasises the grotesqueries of others. Language is used to conceal, to reveal and also to revel in sensational incidents. Jonathan Harker's comment in the first chapter, 'I had all sorts of queer dreams' (p. 4), is an understated introduction to the theme that will recur throughout the novel. This is in contrast to the extravagance of his nightmares in Castle Dracula: 'No man knows till he has suffered from the night how sweet and how dear to his heart and eye the morning can be' (Chapter 4, p. 40). Jonathan's response to his dilemma is to veil his distress with words of restraint. Dr Seward's response later in the novel to Lucy's transformation, the death of his dream of love, is most vivid: 'The sweetness was turned to adamantine, heartless cruelty, and the purity to voluptuous wantonness', and he contemplates her destruction with 'savage delight' (Chapter 16, p. 175).

It is in the descriptions of blood that Stoker revels most in the gore of his horror. The four transfusions to Lucy have their own particular significances, but the vampiric activity is different. Jonathan's shaving cut that has blood 'trickling over my chin' is innocent enough, but for Dracula's reaction (Chapter 2, p. 23). Most of the blood spilt in the novel 'trickles', except for Dracula's blood that Mina sees 'spurt out' (Chapter 21, p. 240), and Quincey Morris's blood that 'gushed' from his fatal wound (Chapter 27, p. 314). Stoker dwells on the stains and trails caused by wounds: Harker finds 'gouts of fresh blood' on Count Dracula in his coffin (Chapter 4, p. 44); Lucy's 'drop of blood' (Chapter 8, p. 78) becomes a 'stream' (Chapter 16, p. 175). As she attacks the children, her lips are 'crimson with fresh blood' (p. 175). When Lucy is destroyed by Arthur, Stoker shows her 'mouth smeared with a crimson foam' (Chapter 16, p. 179).

The staining of clothes and face is a point of similarity between Lucy and Mina. Mina's nightdress, lips, cheeks and chin are all

CONTEXT

In the same year as *Dracula* was published, Rudyard Kipling wrote a poem called 'The Vampire'.

QUESTION
Stoker's range of descriptive vocabulary often seems repetitive. Which words are shared and echoed by the various narrators and what is the effect of this repetition?

equally 'smeared with blood' (Chapter 21, p. 234); Dracula leaves a vivid image of 'the full lips of the blood-dripping mouth' (p. 235); and Jonathan is also 'stained with blood', his wife's blood (p. 236). Renfield, whom we see 'licking up like a dog' (Chapter 11, p. 118) the blood from Dr Seward's wrist wound, dies in a 'glittering pool of blood' (Chapter 21, p. 228). Van Helsing defies the 'lips of bloody foam' to complete the task of destroying the three vampire women (Chapter 27, p. 309).

Van Helsing's imperfect English is in significant contrast to the perfect formulations of Count Dracula. Both characters are men of books and learning, devotees of esoteric knowledge. But the Count is shown to be concerned to master the language just as he wishes to master the new country. His precision in language is a **metaphorical** reflection of his cunning and his will to dominate. Van Helsing's speech, in many ways, is more closely related to the language of the group he leads. Dracula's archaic and book-learnt speech is of another time; Van Helsing recognises his own imperfections in his speech. Thus, Stoker allows his characters' language to convey personal identity, not just in the words they use but in their attitudes to language itself.

PART FOUR

CRITICAL HISTORY

ORIGINAL RECEPTION

Dracula did not win unqualified praise from the critics when published in May 1897. 'Have old beliefs really ceased to impress the imagination?' asked the *Daily News*. The *Manchester Guardian* was quite savage, calling *Dracula* 'an artistic mistake'. The *Observer* found Stoker's choice of subject 'gruesome' and 'one quite unworthy of his literary capabilities', dismissing the story as 'a veritable feast of horrors'. The reviewer in the *Athenaeum* thought it was 'too direct and uncompromising', 'highly sensational', but 'wanting in the constructive art as well as in the higher literary sense'.

The *Pall Mall Gazette* said perhaps more than it realised in suggesting 'Mr. Bram Stoker should have labelled his book "For Strong Men Only," or words to that effect.' Despite thinking it 'horrid and creepy', the reviewer conceded it was 'one of the best things in the supernatural line'.

Others were more enthusiastic still. The *Daily Mail* thought it a 'weird, powerful, and horrorful story … appalling in its gloomy fascination'. And the *Daily Telegraph* praised its 'confident reliance on superstition as furnishing the groundwork of a modern story' and its 'bold adaptation of the legend [of the werewolf] to such ordinary spheres of latter-day existence'. The *Glasgow Herald* and *St James' Gazette* detected the influence of Wilkie Collins on the narrative construction, the former noting that 'as strange event follows strange event, the narrative might in less skilful hands become intolerably improbable'. Both agreed it was Stoker's best book so far.

The *Spectator* was decidedly less impressed and thought 'the sentimental element is decidedly mawkish'. Given that Dracula's direct appearances in the novel are few, it is surprising that one reviewer objected to 'the unnecessary number of hideous incidents recounted of the man-vampire', though Stoker would probably have been pleased with the same *Bookman* reviewer for the statement: 'A summary of the book would shock and disgust'.

> **CONTEXT**
>
> In early drafts of *Dracula, The Dead Undead* was considered by Stoker as a possible title. Just a few weeks before his work was published, the manuscript title was *The Undead*.

Some commentators compared Stoker's novel favourably with the works of widely regarded writers such as Mary Shelley and Edgar Allan Poe.

THE TWENTIETH CENTURY

Bram Stoker did not receive much critical attention until the 1970s. This would tend to suggest that the academic community was unconvinced of the merits of the author or the novel. It should be remembered that the study of English literature was quite a narrow field in comparison with today's pluralist marketplace where the eclectic combination of competing theories is the norm. Devendra P. Varma was one of the relatively few academics making a special study of *Dracula*, its relationship with Gothic literature and the **Romantic** period as a whole. While his work became accepted as something more valuable than an esoteric study on the fringes of the curriculum, the early writings of 'vampirologists' such as Montague Summers have had less sustained critical impact (not least because they tend to believe in the literal truth of 'vampirism').

The 1970s saw a revival of interest in *Dracula* and critical views began to be published from many new literary schools. Marxist, psychoanalytical, feminist and psychosexual approaches all found the text open ground for a variety of readings. Christopher Bentley's 'The Monster in the Bedroom: Sexual Symbolism in Bram Stoker's *Dracula*' and Christopher Craft's '"Kiss Me with Those Red Lips": Gender and Inversion in Bram Stoker's *Dracula*' are often recommended in bibliographies of readings that analyse the issues of gender and sexuality in *Dracula* and give detailed criticism of the homoerotic and inverted gender aspects of the novel's content. Other examples of critical perspectives on gender in *Dracula* include Phyllis A. Roth's 'Suddenly Sexual Women in Bram Stoker's *Dracula*' and Carol A. Senf's '*Dracula*: The Unseen Face in the Mirror'. Stephen D. Arata's 'The Occidental Tourist: *Dracula* and the Anxiety of Reverse Colonialism' gives a post-colonial perspective which draws on another view of the novel's connections to historical and social contexts. The essays by Bentley and Senf can

CHECK THE FILM
Dan Curtis's 1974 *Dracula*, made for television with Jack Palance in the title role, is one of the few adaptations to include references to the historical Vlad Tepes that 1970s academic research had connected directly to Stoker's character Count Dracula.

be found in *Dracula: The Vampire and the Critics*, edited by
Margaret L. Carter; all the other articles have been reprinted in
Dracula: Contemporary Critical Essays, edited by Glennis Byron
(see **Further reading** for more details).

RECENT CRITICAL REVIEWS

The novel attracts interest from diverse academic fields of research,
particularly those connected to psychology, sociology and cultural
studies. Responses to the novel in the last decade or so have
provided much illuminating commentary on the relevance of
Stoker's position as an Irish Protestant writer in exile in London.
Writing in the *London Review of Books* in 2004, Marxist academic
Terry Eagleton provocatively places *Dracula* in a cultural tradition
that was slow to embrace literary realism: 'There is a fertile lineage
of Gothic fiction in Ireland, from Charles Maturin's *Melmoth the
Wanderer* and Sheridan Le Fanu's *Uncle Silas* to Bram Stoker's
Dracula and Oscar Wilde's *The Picture of Dorian Gray*.' This
specifically Irish Gothic tradition was linked, in his view, to the
position of the Irish aristocracy and its relationship with the British
government: 'Stoker's Dracula is that most Irish of villains, an
absentee landlord, who leaves his Transylvanian castle to buy up
property in London.'

There are other academics with a more subtle approach to the novel.
Joseph Valente in his introduction to *Dracula's Crypt: Bram Stoker,
Irishness, and the Question of Blood* (2002) states: 'To treat *Dracula*
as a fantasy on its own terms, then, one must fashion a necessarily
abrasive and unstable synthesis of psychobiographical and cultural
studies approaches to the novel.' Valente gives exhaustive
consideration to the story as an extended analogy of the condition
of Ireland in Stoker's life.

There is also a trend within recent criticism that reacts against what
it sees to be 'over-interpretation'. It has been suggested that much
recent criticism tends to find whatever it may be seeking in this text,
and indeed all texts. The reader brings something to the text; that
much is undeniable. How far some readers take something of the
text into themselves is another matter. It is not at all surprising that

 **CHECK
THE NET**
You can read the
introduction to
Joseph Valente's
*Dracula's Crypt:
Bram Stoker,
Irishness, and the
Question of Blood*
online: go to
**www.press.uillinois.
edu** and search for
'Joseph Valente'.

this novel, which centres itself on questions surrounding the limits of universal knowledge, has attracted so much transcendental commentary. Readers have taken the form of this novel and its paradoxical uncertainties as the basis for complex speculations about its content or meanings. In doing so, they advance their own outlooks, their own prejudices and political views. It is not so strange that this debate polarises into views of Stoker and his novel as 'progressive', 'subversive' or 'reactionary'.

It is not so easy to find a critical voice that provides a balanced view of Stoker, his villain and his novel, and shows them as an intriguing mixture of all these politicised stances. Some writers describe the state of contemporary criticism of Gothic literature as something of a hideous ruin. If we leave to one side the titanic struggles between good and evil it contains, the novel *Dracula* is now an ideological battleground for academics offering a variety of creative interpretations.

However, the old literary tradition – the elitist appraisal of effectiveness, leading to qualitative judgement of writing per se – seems to be the undead literary monster haunting the battlefield. Instead of an implied hierarchy of texts, or canon, which privileged some readers, is there now an implied hierarchy of textual readings which does much the same thing but in a different way? Entering this conflicted arena of critical debate, it is no bad thing to be 'a stranger, without prejudice, and with the habit of keeping an open mind', as Van Helsing recommends (Chapter 18, p. 204).

CONTEXT

Count Dracula has an extraordinary intertextual presence in children's literature and television. The generation brought up on *Sesame Street* will remember Count von Count (based on Bela Lugosi's iconic interpretation of the character).

PART FIVE

BACKGROUND

BRAM STOKER

Bram Stoker was born in 1847 in Clontarf, near Dublin, Ireland. His father was a civil servant and Bram was the third child of seven in a middle-class, Protestant family. Stoker suffered ill health as a child and spent much of his childhood confined to his bed. He recovered and went on to study at Trinity College in Dublin, where he successfully competed in athletics. He was involved in Trinity College's Philosophical Society and participated in the social life beyond the university.

For ten years or so, Bram Stoker worked as a civil servant in Dublin Castle. He was passionate about serious theatre and his enthusiasm for the performances of Henry Irving, the leading Shakespearian actor of the time, led to him becoming an amateur theatre critic. He then married Florence Balcombe and moved to London to become the manager of Irving's Lyceum Theatre; he wrote his stories and novels while still working in the theatre. Stoker had many friends and acquaintances in the literary world, including Arthur Conan Doyle, Alfred Tennyson and Mark Twain. His friendship with Oscar Wilde and the American poet Walt Whitman has caused speculation about Stoker's personal sexuality, despite a lack of biographical detail.

Stoker's later life was not particularly happy. The Lyceum Theatre suffered a fire that forced Irving to start touring the country again; and Irving died in 1905. Stoker became seriously ill after Irving's death and he spent the last few years of his life in reduced financial circumstances. He did not live to enjoy the great success of his most well-known work.

OTHER WORKS

Stoker wrote thirteen novels between 1875 and 1911. *Dracula* is usually considered his best work, though at the time he won greater fame as the biographer of Henry Irving. His *Personal Reminiscences*

CHECK THE BOOK

For more biographical detail read Barbara Belford's *Bram Stoker: A Biography of the Author of Dracula* (1996).

CONTEXT

Henry Irving (1838–1905) was the first English actor to receive a knighthood. He made his London acting debut in 1866 at the St James's Theatre; in 1871 he transferred to the Lyceum, and earned the reputation as the greatest English actor of his time. His theatrical partnership with actress Ellen Terry began in 1878, and lasted until 1902.

CHECK THE FILM

The Jewel of Seven Stars was filmed as The Awakening in 1980, directed by Mike Newell and starring Charlton Heston and Susannah York, while Ken Russell directed The Lair of the White Worm in 1988.

CHECK THE NET

You can read The Jewel of Seven Stars and The Lair of the White Worm online at www.online-literature.com

CHECK THE BOOK

In Northanger Abbey Jane Austen parodies the taste for Gothic fiction. The heroine's judgement is somewhat skewed by an overly assiduous reading of Ann Radcliffe's novels, and she imagines a mystery where there is none.

of *Henry Irving* was published in two volumes in 1906. In the novel *The Snake's Pass*, published in 1890, Stoker deals most openly with the political context of Ireland. His later novels with supernatural elements – *The Jewel of Seven Stars*, published in 1903, about a cursed Egyptian mummy; and *The Lair of the White Worm*, published in 1911, based on medieval legends of enormous snakes – have both been adapted for the cinema.

Stoker wrote many short stories over the course of his career. His collection of stories written for children, *Under the Sunset*, was published in 1882. Although children's literature can and does feature many gruesome episodes, these dark tales are not highly regarded. *Dracula's Guest*, a collection published after Stoker's death by his widow, is most notable for the story written for, but edited out of, the final version of *Dracula*. Bram Stoker had a dozen or so more short stories published during his life, which have not, so far, been gathered into a collected edition. He also wrote some works of non-fiction, of which *The Duties of Clerks of Petty Sessions in Ireland*, based on his work in the civil service and published in 1879, is the most well known. One of the papers Stoker presented to the University Philosophical Society had the title 'Sensationalism in Fiction and Society'.

LITERARY BACKGROUND

THE GOTHIC TRADITION

Horace Walpole's *The Castle of Otranto* (1765), Ann Radcliffe's *The Mysteries of Udolpho* (1794) and Matthew G. Lewis's *The Monk* (1796) are considered to be the 'classic' Gothic tales that established the **conventions** of the **genre** in English literature. The characters tend to be rather two-dimensional, suffering excesses of emotional stress through fear and terror, mostly related to supernatural phenomena, and the events take place in unfamiliar locations distanced in time from the present moment.

Jane Austen's *Northanger Abbey* (begun in 1798 and published posthumously in 1818) shifted the focus of the genre from the perceived hysteria of the victim, as caused by external intimidation, to the psychological interior world of her characters.

Some commentators see this as a response to the waning credibility of the Gothic convention, though the popularity of horrific and sensational stories seemed undiminished in the burgeoning mass culture. Mary Shelley's *Frankenstein*, which appeared in 1818, relies so little on the traditionally identified elements of the Gothic tale that it almost appears to be outside the genre altogether.

The Gothic sensibility in literature is seen by some as an attempt to deal with the feared and unknown consequences of social change. Sensational thrills are provided by the characters going beyond the boundaries of acceptable behaviour. The challenge to the normal conduct of society and individuals often ends unhappily for the protagonist.

But the genre is not limited to questions of moral or ethical imprudence. The later Victorian Gothic novels explore the darker aspects of the human psyche in the familiar setting of the modern world. This is a conscious attempt to question, by bringing the terrors of the past into conflict with the assumed certainties of the present, the direction of social progress. Robert Louis Stevenson's *The Strange Case of Dr Jekyll and Mr Hyde* (1886) and Oscar Wilde's *The Picture of Dorian Gray* (1890) use the notion of multiple personality to explore the dual nature of humanity as man-beast, god-devil, angel-demon. As in H. G. Wells's *The Island of Doctor Moreau* (1896), science and religion are called into question as the authors dwell on the potential horrors and glories within the individual. In this way they reflect the powerful revolutionary changes taking place in the nineteenth century that still inspire and influence our understanding of personal identity and social responsibility.

THE VAMPIRE IN LITERATURE

The figure of the vampire is an international phenomenon found in the legends of many cultures. Scholars have identified a wide-ranging variety of influences combined in the literary realisation of this monster.

The German poet Goethe in 1797 in *The Bride of Corinth* gave the vampire some of the classical weight of ancient Greek mythology, while Samuel Taylor Coleridge's poem 'Christabel' (1816) is taken

CHECK THE BOOK

For a short essay on Gothic fiction, see *The Oxford Companion to English Literature* (sixth edition, edited by Margaret Drabble).

THE VAMPIRE IN LITERATURE continued

CONTEXT

Lake Leman near Geneva was the setting for a famous literary rendezvous. Percy Bysshe Shelley, Mary Shelley, Claire Clairmont and Polidori were being entertained by Lord Byron in 1816. In response to Byron's challenge to write a supernatural story, Mary Shelley created *Frankenstein*. Shortly afterwards, Polidori wrote 'The Vampyre', which seems to have been intended as a weirdly flattering portrait of Byron's reputation for excessive behaviour. It is an appropriately romantic coincidence that the genesis of two enduring cultural icons, Frankenstein's monster and the vampire, can be traced to the same moment.

to be the first appearance of the vampire in English literature. John William Polidori, Lord Byron's companion, published 'The Vampyre' in instalments in Henry Colburn's *New Monthly Magazine* in 1819 (although he wrote the story in 1816). It is said that Polidori found his inspiration in the same German Gothic tales that inspired Mary Shelley to write *Frankenstein*. Vampire plays in the theatre were particularly popular in Paris around this time: Alexandre Dumas wrote his play *Le Vampire* in 1851.

Varney the Vampire: Or the Feast of Blood, usually attributed to Thomas Preskett Prest, author of *Sweeny Todd, the Demon Barber of Fleet Street*, was also published first in instalments (1845–7). *Varney* was printed in a complete volume in 1847. The female vampire in 'Carmilla', a story published in the collection entitled *In a Glass Darkly* by Joseph Sheridan Le Fanu in 1872, is the first example of the thread of fantasised lesbian eroticism that features so readily in the cinema adaptations of the legend. *Dracula*, in some perspectives, presents a robustly heterosexual response to this feminised tale.

HISTORICAL BACKGROUND

THE END OF AN ERA

Dracula was written at the time of Britain's supremacy as a world power. For much of the nineteenth century, Britain's industrial strength dominated the international marketplace. The technological advances of the preceding decades were shrinking the world and creating communication channels of such rapidity that the social understanding of time and space was being fundamentally altered. In every field of human endeavour, from medicine to engineering to commerce, it seemed to be a golden age of advancement and progress. Or at least that is how the Victorian middle class liked to view their world. For nations under British rule, or for the working class in Britain, the story is more truthfully told as a struggle to gain rights and semi-respectable conditions for life.

In 1897, the year of the Diamond Jubilee, the official celebration of her sixty years as queen and empress, Victoria was already confined to a wheelchair. It was obvious that her long reign could not go on for ever. Her son and heir, Edward, had a well-established reputation as a decadent playboy. The future of the monarchy was not necessarily in safe hands.

After a turbulent period of revolutions in the middle of the century that recalled the heady days of the French Revolution, the movement towards greater participation in democracy was being tightly controlled. The power of the new urban working class through its organisation in trade unions presented, to some Victorian statesmen, the threat of the mob and the guillotine. While trade union members were no longer transported to the penal colonies, the suppression of the unions was continued through legal devices that effectively made it impossible for them to function. Out of this struggle the Labour Party would be created, formed explicitly to represent the working class in the democratic process.

British sovereignty was being contested in the further reaches of the empire and closer to home. One of the results of a wider franchise was to bring forward the question of British governance of Ireland. The Liberal Party, which introduced electoral reform, found itself divided absolutely over the question of Home Rule. The end of the century was anticipated with suspense and anticipation. Many men born in the year of *Dracula*'s publication would grow up to fight and to perish in the mechanised bloodbath of the First World War.

CHECK THE FILM

Carl Dreyer's 1932 film *Vampyr* was based on Sheridan Le Fanu's story 'Carmilla'. It has been called 'one of the greatest of horror films'; David Thomson in *The New Biographical Dictionary of Film* (2002) goes on to say that 'Without ever discarding the Gothic elements of vampirism, it sees in its subject a universal emotional encounter.'

CHECK THE BOOK

See *A Companion to Victorian Literature and Culture* (1999), edited by Herbert F. Tucker, for a good working introduction to the period.

World events	Bram Stoker's life	Literary events
1802 Development of steam locomotive		
		1813 Lord Byron, *The Giaour*
1818 First successful human blood transfusions at Guy's Hospital, London		**1818** Mary Shelley, *Frankenstein, or The Modern Prometheus*
1819 Birth of future Queen Victoria		**1819** John William Polidori's 'The Vampyre' published
1832 First Reform Act increases electorate to about half a million		
1837 Queen Victoria's coronation; first telegraphic communication		
1838 The People's Charter published as start of the Chartist movement for political reform		
		1839 Edgar Allan Poe, 'The Fall of the House of Usher'
	1847 Born 8 November at Clontarf near Dublin	**1847** *Varney the Vampire* published; Charlotte Brontë, *Jane Eyre*
	1847–54 First seven years troubled by ill health	
1848 Karl Marx and Friedrich Engels publish the *Communist Manifesto*; Pre-Raphaelite Brotherhood formed by Dante Gabriel Rossetti, William Holman Hunt and Sir John Everett Millais		**1848** Emily Brontë, *Wuthering Heights*
1851 Great Exhibition at Crystal Palace, Hyde Park		**1851** Alexandre Dumas, *Le Vampire*
1853 The hypodermic syringe is introduced		
		1855 Walt Whitman, *Leaves of Grass*

World events	Bram Stoker's life	Literary events
		1859 John Stuart Mill, *On Liberty*; Charles Darwin, *On the Origin of Species by Means of Natural Selection*
		1860 Wilkie Collins, *The Woman in White*
1861–5 American Civil War		
	1863 Studies at Trinity College, University of Dublin; president of the University Philosophical Society	
		1864–5 Charles Dickens, *Our Mutual Friend*
		1865 Lewis Carroll, *Alice in Wonderland*
1867 Second Reform Act doubles electorate from 1 million to 2 million; Karl Marx publishes first volume of *Das Kapital*	**1869** Becomes amateur theatre critic for *Dublin Evening Mail* and editor of *Irish Echo*	**1869** John Stuart Mill, *On the Subjection of Women*
1870 Elementary Education Act introduces School Boards	**1870** Employed as a civil servant in Dublin Castle	
1871 Trade unions granted legal status; population of Britain now c.26 million		
	1872 First story 'The Crystal Cup' published	**1872** Joseph Sheridan Le Fanu, *In a Glass Darkly* (collection of stories which includes 'Carmilla')
	1875 'The Chain of Destiny' serialised in four parts in *The Shamrock*	**1875** Anthony Trollope, *The Way We Live Now*
1876 Queen Victoria proclaimed Empress of India	**1876** Meets Henry Irving in Dublin	**1876** Mark Twain, *The Adventures of Tom Sawyer*

World events

1877 Thomas Edison produces the phonograph

1879 Edison invents electric light bulb

1880–1 First Boer War

1882 Married Women's Property Act

1884 Third Reform Act triples the electorate to *c*.6 million

1885 Age of sexual consent for girls raised to sixteen; new penalties for male homosexuality implemented in Criminal Law Amendment Act

1886 Home Rule for Ireland rejected

1887–8 Queen Victoria's Golden Jubilee; Jack the Ripper murders six women in London

Bram Stoker's life

1878 Begins work as secretary and manager for Henry Irving at Lyceum Theatre, London; marries Florence Balcombe

1879 *The Duties of Clerks of Petty Sessions in Ireland*; birth of son, Noel

1882 *Under the Sunset*, a collection of tales for children

1884 Meets Walt Whitman, American poet

1886 *A Glimpse of America*, travel writings

1890 First full-length novel *The Snake's Pass*; begins research notes for vampire story; called to the Bar, but never practises as barrister

Literary events

1878 Thomas Hardy, *The Return of the Native*

1879 Henrik Ibsen, *A Doll's House*

1886 Robert Louis Stevenson, *The Strange Case of Dr Jekyll and Mr Hyde*

1890 Oscar Wilde, *The Picture of Dorian Gray*

1891 William Morris, *News from Nowhere*

1892 Sigmund Freud, *A Case of a Successful Treatment by Hypnotism*; Arthur Conan Doyle, *The Adventures of Sherlock Holmes*

World events	Bram Stoker's life	Literary events
		1895 Trial and conviction of Oscar Wilde for 'gross indecency' – imprisoned for two years
1896 The Lumière brothers' cinematograph presents first projected film in London		**1896** H. G. Wells, *The Island of Doctor Moreau*
1897 Queen Victoria's Diamond Jubilee	**1897** First dramatised reading of *Dracula* at Lyceum; *Dracula* published	
		1898 H. G. Wells, *The War of the Worlds*
1899–1902 Second Boer War	**1899** First US publication of *Dracula*	
1901 Death of Queen Victoria		**1901** Rudyard Kipling, *Kim*
	1902 *The Mystery of the Sea*	
	1903 *The Jewel of Seven Stars*	
1905 Henry Irving dies; revolution in Russia		**1905** George Bernard Shaw, *Major Barbara*
	1906 *Personal Reminiscences of Henry Irving*	
	1909 *The Lady of the Shroud*	
	1911 *The Lair of the White Worm*	
	1912 Dies on 20 April aged sixty-four	
		1913 D. H. Lawrence, *Sons and Lovers*
1914–18 First World War	**1914** *Dracula's Guest*, a collection of stories, published posthumously by Florence Stoker	

FURTHER READING

Nina Auerbach, *Our Vampires, Ourselves*, Chicago: University of Chicago Press, 1995

Barbara Belford, *Bram Stoker: A Biography of the Author of Dracula*, New York: Alfred A. Knopf, 1996

Alok Bhalla, *Politics of Atrocity and Lust: The Vampire Tale as a Nightmare History of England in the Nineteenth Century*, New Delhi: Sterling, 1990

Matthew C. Brennan, *The Gothic Psyche: Disintegration and Growth in Nineteenth-Century English Literature*, Columbia, SC: Camden House, 1997

Glennis Byron (ed.), *Dracula: Contemporary Critical Essays*, New Casebooks, London: Macmillan, 1999
> Includes essays by Phyllis A. Roth, Christopher Craft, Stephen D. Arata, Nina Auerbach and Franco Moretti

Margaret L. Carter (ed.), *Dracula: The Vampire and the Critics*, Ann Arbor: University of Michigan Press, 1988
> Includes Christopher Bentley's essay 'The Monster in the Bedroom: Sexual Symbolism in Bram Stoker's *Dracula*' and Carol A. Senf's '*Dracula*: The Unseen Face in the Mirror'

Bram Dijkstra, *Idols of Perversity: Fantasies of Feminine Evil in Fin-de-Siècle Culture*, Oxford: Oxford University Press, 1987

Margaret Drabble (ed.), *The Oxford Companion to English Literature*, Oxford: Oxford University Press, sixth edition, 2000

Radu R. Florescu and Raymond T. McNally, *Dracula: Prince of Many Faces*, Boston: Little, Brown and Company, 1989

Christopher Frayling, *Vampyres: Lord Byron to Count Dracula*, London: Faber and Faber, 1991

Brian J. Frost, *The Monster with a Thousand Faces: Guises of the Vampire in Myth and Literature*, Bowling Green, OH: Bowling Green State University Popular Press, 1989

Ken Gelder, *Reading the Vampire*, London: Routledge, 1994

Sandra M. Gilbert and Susan Gubar, *The Madwoman in the Attic: The Woman Writer and the Nineteenth-Century Literary Imagination*, New Haven: Yale University Press, 1979

David Glover, *Vampires, Mummies, and Liberals: Bram Stoker and the Politics of Popular Fiction*, Durham: Duke University Press, 1966

James Craig Holte, *Dracula in the Dark: The Dracula Film Adaptations*, Westport, CT: Greenwood Press, 1997

William Hughes and Andrew Smith (eds.), *Bram Stoker: History, Psychoanalysis and the Gothic*, London: Macmillan, 1998

Richard Jacobs, *A Beginner's Guide to Critical Reading: Readings for Students*, London: Routledge, 2001

P. J. Keating, *The Working Classes in Victorian Fiction*, London: Routledge, 1971

Salli J. Kline, *The Degeneration of Women: Bram Stoker's Dracula as Allegorical Criticism of the Fin de Siècle*, Rheinbach-Merzbach: CMZ-Verlag, 1992

Clive Leatherdale, *Dracula: The Novel and the Legend*, London: Desert Island Books, 1993

Michael McKeon (ed.), *Theory of the Novel: A Historical Approach*, Baltimore: Johns Hopkins Press, 2000

H. L. Malchow, *Gothic Images of Race in Nineteenth-Century Britain*, Stanford: Stanford University Press, 1996

Michael Mason, *The Making of Victorian Sexuality*, Oxford: Oxford University Press, 1994

Robert Mighall, *A Geography of Victorian Gothic Fiction: Mapping History's Nightmares*, Oxford: Oxford University Press, 1999

Elizabeth Miller, *Dracula: Sense & Nonsense*, Westcliff-on-Sea: Desert Island Books, 2000

Franco Moretti, *Signs Taken for Wonders: Essays in the Sociology of Literary Forms*, translated by Susan Fischer, David Forgacs and David Miller, New York: Verso, 1988

Paul Murray, *From the Shadow of Dracula: A Life of Bram Stoker*, London: Jonathan Cape, 2004

Barbara Onslow, *Women of the Press in Nineteenth-Century Britain*, New York: St. Martin's Press, 2000

FURTHER READING

Carol A. Senf, *The Vampire in Nineteenth-Century English Literature*, Bowling Green, OH: Bowling Green State University Popular Press, 1988

Carol A. Senf, *Dracula: Between Tradition and Modernism*, New York: Twayne Publishers, 1998

Carol A. Senf, *Science and Social Science in Bram Stoker's Fiction*, Westport, CT: Greenwood Press, 2002

Carol A. Senf (ed.), *The Critical Response to Bram Stoker*, Westport, CT: Greenwood Press, 1993

David J. Skal, *Hollywood Gothic: The Tangled Web of Dracula from Novel to Stage to Screen*, New York: Norton, 1990 (revised 2004)

Andrew Smith (ed.), *Dracula and the Critics*, Sheffield: Pavic, 1996

Roxana Stuart, *Stage Blood: Vampires of the Nineteenth-Century Stage*, Bowling Green, OH: Bowling Green State University Popular Press, 1994

Herbert F. Tucker (ed.), *A Companion to Victorian Literature and Culture*, Oxford: Blackwell, 1999

James Twitchell, *The Living Dead: A Study of the Vampire in Romantic Literature*, Durham, NC: Duke University Press, 1981

Joseph Valente, *Dracula's Crypt: Bram Stoker, Irishness, and the Question of Blood*, Champaign, IL: University of Illinois Press, 2002

allegory a form of extended **metaphor**. Things and people are representative **symbols** and not necessarily intended to be literally understood

ambivalence uncertainty or contradictory meaning or attitudes

antithesis an opposite to something

archetype the original, the pattern to be copied

atmosphere a term, open to interpretation, that tries to describe the effect at the moment of realisation of the text

convention the common features in texts that are said to identify a particular literary form. They are related to readers' expectations and cultural trends

exposition the explanation of events or demonstration of the meaning of events

genre a literary type or style of text

imagery language used that creates sensations for the reader

irony a sense of the often ridiculous contrast between intended outcome and actuality

melodrama highly exaggerated emotion and simplicity of moral attitudes

metaphor a comparison that carries meaning about one thing in the form of another thing

narrative perspective the point of view of the person telling the story

narrator the character telling the story, not the author

personification a form of **metaphor**, abstract qualities given human form or a person typifying a quality

Romantic related to the Romantic movement of the late eighteenth century and early nineteenth century that idealised nature

symbol a thing that represents something else either directly or indirectly

tableau a theatrical description for a still scene more often described in cinematic terms as 'freeze-frame'

theme a dominant idea or concept that recurs throughout a text

tone an imprecise term, used to indicate mood or **atmosphere**

AUTHOR OF THESE NOTES

Steve Roberts is a Senior Lecturer in English at the University of Brighton and a former Head of English at secondary level. He has a degree in English and Drama from Goldsmiths College, University of London, and worked in the theatre before becoming a teacher.

Maya Angelou
I Know Why the Caged Bird Sings

Jane Austen
Pride and Prejudice

Alan Ayckbourn
Absent Friends

Elizabeth Barrett Browning
Selected Poems

Robert Bolt
A Man for All Seasons

Harold Brighouse
Hobson's Choice

Charlotte Brontë
Jane Eyre

Emily Brontë
Wuthering Heights

Brian Clark
Whose Life is it Anyway?

Robert Cormier
Heroes

Shelagh Delaney
A Taste of Honey

Charles Dickens
David Copperfield
Great Expectations
Hard Times
Oliver Twist
Selected Stories

Roddy Doyle
Paddy Clarke Ha Ha Ha

George Eliot
Silas Marner
The Mill on the Floss

Anne Frank
The Diary of a Young Girl

William Golding
Lord of the Flies

Oliver Goldsmith
She Stoops to Conquer

Willis Hall
The Long and the Short and the Tall

Thomas Hardy
Far from the Madding Crowd
The Mayor of Casterbridge
Tess of the d'Urbervilles
The Withered Arm and other Wessex Tales

L. P. Hartley
The Go-Between

Seamus Heaney
Selected Poems

Susan Hill
I'm the King of the Castle

Barry Hines
A Kestrel for a Knave

Louise Lawrence
Children of the Dust

Harper Lee
To Kill a Mockingbird

Laurie Lee
Cider with Rosie

Arthur Miller
The Crucible
A View from the Bridge

Robert O'Brien
Z for Zachariah

Frank O'Connor
My Oedipus Complex and Other Stories

George Orwell
Animal Farm

J. B. Priestley
An Inspector Calls
When We Are Married

Willy Russell
Educating Rita
Our Day Out

J. D. Salinger
The Catcher in the Rye

William Shakespeare
Henry IV Part I
Henry V
Julius Caesar
Macbeth
The Merchant of Venice
A Midsummer Night's Dream
Much Ado About Nothing
Romeo and Juliet
The Tempest
Twelfth Night

George Bernard Shaw
Pygmalion

Mary Shelley
Frankenstein

R. C. Sherriff
Journey's End

Rukshana Smith
Salt on the snow

John Steinbeck
Of Mice and Men

Robert Louis Stevenson
Dr Jekyll and Mr Hyde

Jonathan Swift
Gulliver's Travels

Robert Swindells
Daz 4 Zoe

Mildred D. Taylor
Roll of Thunder, Hear My Cry

Mark Twain
Huckleberry Finn

James Watson
Talking in Whispers

Edith Wharton
Ethan Frome

William Wordsworth
Selected Poems

A Choice of Poets

Mystery Stories of the Nineteenth Century including The Signalman

Nineteenth Century Short Stories

Poetry of the First World War

Six Women Poets

For the AQA Anthology:

Duffy and Armitage & Pre-1914 Poetry

Heaney and Clarke & Pre-1914 Poetry

Poems from Different Cultures

Margaret Atwood
Cat's Eye
The Handmaid's Tale

Jane Austen
Emma
Mansfield Park
Persuasion
Pride and Prejudice
Sense and Sensibility

William Blake
*Songs of Innocence and of
Experience*

Charlotte Brontë
Jane Eyre
Villette

Emily Brontë
Wuthering Heights

Angela Carter
Nights at the Circus
Wise Children

Geoffrey Chaucer
The Franklin's Prologue and Tale
The Miller's Prologue and Tale
*The Prologue to the Canterbury
Tales*
*The Wife of Bath's Prologue and
Tale*

Samuel Coleridge
Selected Poems

Joseph Conrad
Heart of Darkness

Daniel Defoe
Moll Flanders

Charles Dickens
Bleak House
Great Expectations
Hard Times

Emily Dickinson
Selected Poems

John Donne
Selected Poems

Carol Ann Duffy
Selected Poems

George Eliot
Middlemarch
The Mill on the Floss

T. S. Eliot
Selected Poems
The Waste Land

F. Scott Fitzgerald
The Great Gatsby

E. M. Forster
A Passage to India

Charles Frazier
Cold Mountain

Brian Friel
Translations
Making History

William Golding
The Spire

Thomas Hardy
Jude the Obscure
The Mayor of Casterbridge
The Return of the Native
Selected Poems
Tess of the d'Urbervilles

Seamus Heaney
*Selected Poems from 'Opened
Ground'*

Nathaniel Hawthorne
The Scarlet Letter

Homer
The Iliad
The Odyssey

Aldous Huxley
Brave New World

Kazuo Ishiguro
The Remains of the Day

Ben Jonson
The Alchemist

James Joyce
Dubliners

John Keats
Selected Poems

Christopher Marlowe
Doctor Faustus
Edward II

Ian McEwan
Atonement

Arthur Miller
Death of a Salesman

John Milton
Paradise Lost Books I & II

Toni Morrison
Beloved

George Orwell
Nineteen Eighty-Four

Sylvia Plath
Selected Poems

Alexander Pope
*Rape of the Lock & Selected
Poems*

William Shakespeare
Antony and Cleopatra
As You Like It
Hamlet
Henry IV Part I
King Lear
Macbeth
Measure for Measure
The Merchant of Venice
A Midsummer Night's Dream
Much Ado About Nothing
Othello
Richard II
Richard III
Romeo and Juliet
The Taming of the Shrew
The Tempest
Twelfth Night
The Winter's Tale

George Bernard Shaw
Saint Joan

Mary Shelley
Frankenstein

Bram Stoker
Dracula

Jonathan Swift
*Gulliver's Travels and A Modest
Proposal*

Alfred Tennyson
Selected Poems

Alice Walker
The Color Purple

Oscar Wilde
*The Importance of Being
Earnest*

Tennessee Williams
A Streetcar Named Desire

Jeanette Winterson
Oranges Are Not the Only Fruit

John Webster
The Duchess of Malfi

Virginia Woolf
To the Lighthouse

W. B. Yeats
Selected Poems

Metaphysical Poets